RELIGIOUS MYSTERY
AND RATIONAL REFLECTION

Religious Mystery and Rational Reflection

Excursions in the Phenomenology and Philosophy of Religion

LOUIS DUPRÉ

William B. Eerdmans Publishing Company
Grand Rapids, Michigan / Cambridge, U.K.

© 1998 Wm. B. Eerdmans Publishing Co.
255 Jefferson Ave. S.E., Grand Rapids, Michigan 49503 /
P.O. Box 163, Cambridge CB3 9PU U.K.

Printed in the United States of America

03 02 01 00 99 98   7 6 5 4 3 2 1

Library of Congress Cataloging-in-Publication Data

Dupré, Louis
Religious mystery and rational reflection / Louis Dupré
p.   cm.
Includes bibliographical references.
ISBN 0-8028-4325-5 (pbk.)
1. Religion — Philosophy.   2. Religion.
3. Symbolism.   4. Experience (Religion)   I. Title.
BL51.D86   1998
200 — dc21   97-24216
CIP

Contents

Acknowledgments

The author and publisher would like to thank the original publishers of the essays here collected for their permission to include them, in reworked and shortened form, in the present volume: *The American Catholic Philosophical Quarterly* for "Phenomenology of Religion" (1992); the State University of New York Press for "The Truth of Religion" (originally published in *The Truth Proper to Religion* [1990], ed. R. Guerrière) and "Ritual and Time" (originally published in *Play, Literature, Religion* [1992], ed. V. Nemoianu and R. Royal); *Faith and Philosophy* for "Philosophy and the Mystery of Evil" (1990); *Communio* for "Religious Symbolism and Aesthetic Form" (1989); The Catholic University Press for "Symbols and Negative Theology" (1980; originally published in part in *Experience, Reason and God*, ed. Eugene Long); *Theological Studies* for "Experience and Interpretation" (1980); *The Journal of Religion* (University of Chicago Press) for "The Christian Experience of Mystical Union" (1989); and *Daedalus,* Journal of the American Academy of Arts and Sciences, for "Spiritual Life in a Secular Age" (1982).

Introduction

The essays here offered were conceived separately, yet originated as different stages of a continuous reflection on the human response to an essentially ungraspable mystery. Most of them have, in slightly different form, appeared in a variety of journals and collective works. In all of them I discuss themes that I consider central to a rational understanding of the phenomenon of religion. Their approach differs from the conceptual and linguistic analysis common in philosophical journals in the English language. Though fully admitting the need for an analytic method in the philosophical study of religion, I believe that a phenomenological description of the primeval experience as well as a critical interpretation of the nature of symbolic activity is indispensable and often neglected. Still too many consider the notion of truth in religion to be a simple one, and not basically different from the scientific one. This may easily lead to mistaken, literalist interpretations of the religious act and its expressions. In addition, the analysis of religious concepts needs to be complemented by a reflection on the religious *experience*. What occupied a place of honor in James's *Varieties of Religious Experience,* the first critical American reflection on religion, namely, the mystical experience, today rarely receives the philosophical attention it deserves. In the essays here presented I have concentrated on symbolization and experience, particularly on the spiritual experience that plays such an essential part in the religious act that the act could not survive without it.

The assumption underlying this investigation is that the religious act comprises two essential components: objective symbolization and subjective experience. To isolate the experience, as some romantic thinkers did, results in a loss of objective content. On the other side, restricting the religious content to a set of objective social symbols, as earlier sociologists and cultural anthropologists used to do, leaves us nothing but the scaffolding of the living act. Only when considering the two components as intrinsically united can philosophy grasp the intentionality proper to the religious act. To do so imposes certain conditions. It requires a careful phenomenological description of the act as well as a full awareness of the distinctive kind of truth the act pursues.

The essays here included vary in method and in purpose. They move rather freely from philosophical argument to phenomenological description to philosophical theology. The nature of religious truth as discussed in Part 1 should at least in part justify the variety of these approaches in the same collection. The encounter with divine transcendence inevitably leads reflection beyond the conceptions of truth as correspondence and coherence that have dominated philosophical thought until recently. Nothing illustrates this as forcefully as the presence of evil, the most pressing mystery of existence and, as Schopenhauer called it, the *crux philosophorum*. No rational reflection, even within the terms of a theistic philosophy, has ever succeeded in justifying it, despite the confident efforts of each new philosophical generation to do so. The philosophical quest for truth, it seems, *either* must erase a discussion of this issue from its agenda as falling beyond the limits of rational knowledge and hence as meaningless, *or* must give up its full autonomy and lower its ambition to exploring the *meaning* that religious traditions over the centuries have found in the very mystery. The boundaries Kant so strictly drew around the field of "philosophical truth" must be crossed if "philosophy" is to make sense of religion at all. (Kant himself crossed them in his *Religion Within the Limits of Reason Alone!*) I can, of course, hardly expect this view to be acceptable to positivists — secular or religious. But other thinkers of our time have freely embraced it — Jaspers, Gadamer, Blondel, and, indirectly, even Heidegger. Nor did medieval thought know the tight compartmentalization by which the moderns have isolated philosophy from theology.

Part 2 shifts the focus to the particular problem of religious symbolism. The most basic category in this area, that of symbolic form, leads directly to the question of religious "aesthetics," masterfully treated by Hans Urs von Balthasar. Next, I turn to that religious form which has often been singled out as the most universal: ritual. All thinking about God results in some form of negative theology. How does that affect the very possibility of religious symbols? This question I discuss in the final essay of Part 2.

Part 3 is devoted to the religious experience. Often we oppose experience to interpretation. But all experience is interpreted by the person who experiences. When the object of the experience is induced by a transcendent revelation, the question occurs how the subjective experience and the reception of an objective message are related in the religious act. I try to answer it in my first essay. In the next one I discuss the religious experience *par excellence,* the mystical awareness of an immediate, divine presence. I have limited the description of the mystical experience to monotheistic religion. The collection concludes with an attempt to assess the possibility of spiritual experience within a thoroughly secular modern culture.

The technical level of the chapters differs. The attempt to justify the method here employed required the rather specialized philosophical discussion of the first two chapters. The others were written with the general, educated reader in mind.

My sincere thanks to the publisher, William B. Eerdmans Jr., and to his staff for their competency and uncommon patience.

PART 1

Questions of Method

Phenomenology of Religion: Limits and Possibilities

For various reasons the time appears ripe for a reconsideration of the phenomenology of religion. After a period of intense interest, begun with Scheler and Van der Leeuw and concluded with Eliade and Duméry, a silence of exhaustion has fallen over the subject, barely disturbed during the last quarter of a century. The decline of interest partly may be due to the fact that those who practiced the phenomenological description most successfully — particularly Van der Leeuw and Eliade — totally sidestepped the ontological problems in an area where those problems were most pressing. Their comparative analyses of religious phenomena are unquestionably inspired by Husserl's phenomenological description, but they seldom surpass the empirical level of an anthropological typology and rarely attain the philosophical justification Husserl required. The eidetic *epochē* here turns into refusal to enter into any problems that exceed description and classification. Still, those who, even during Husserl's lifetime, initiated the phenomenological study of religion knew that more than description was expected. Already in his 1926 *Phénoménologie et philosophie religieuse*[1] Jean Hering directly addressed the methodological issues. And so did Max Scheler in his memorable analysis of the religious act in *On the Eternal in Man*. But, unlike the comparatists Van der Leeuw and Eliade, neither Scheler nor Hering sufficiently recognized the cultural variety of those symbolic expressions through which the religious act intends the transcendent "object." Their work suffers from an abstract gener-

---

1. I found it, partly read, in Husserl's own library in Leuven.

3

alization. Are we truly justified in attributing the common Western name "religion" to that endless variety of activities, mythologies, rituals, and beliefs held and practiced by humans since the beginning of the species? Or do they display merely a vague resemblance between intentional acts that fulfill essentially different functions and intend different "objects"? These questions were not even raised, and it should not surprise us that anthropologists and ethnologists remain skeptical about the early phenomenological investigations.

One phenomenologist, it must be said, went to the heart of the philosophical issue, namely, the active part played by the transcendental ego and its concrete, symbolic expression in the theories, images, and practices of living religion. Henry Duméry limited his study to the single case of Christianity, but carefully explored it in theological and historical detail. Yet outside of French-speaking academic circles, his work never received the attention it deserved. The neglect may partly be due to problems he created for himself by capping his transcendental phenomenology with a Neoplatonic, negative theology of the Absolute — thereby alienating theologians as well as orthodox Husserlians. But equally responsible was the highly technical, idealist vocabulary, grating on the Anglo-American ear, in which he couched his ideas. I will discuss his work in the second section.

Today several factors invite us to reexamine the foundations of a method to which many students in the area of religion continue to pay lip-service but of which few care to justify the application. Philosophy, once again, has begun to take seriously what Husserl, in a conversation with his student Ingarden, called "undoubtedly its most important problem," namely, that of God. Also, the interreligious dialogue, as well as the increasing significance of the academic study of religion, has revived the interest in a more fundamental phenomenological investigation. Finally, attacks on "the epistemological prejudice" of modern philosophy place the concept of religious truth in a new light.

I

The title of this chapter suggests that the possibility of phenomenological philosophy for reflecting on the religious act may be restricted by certain conditions. Three relations in particular need to be clarified for establishing the title's appropriateness: (1) the relation between the psycho-empirical religious experience and its transcendent object; (2) the relation between the transcendental reduction, on the one hand, and the *givenness* of a transcendent revelation, on the other; and (3) the relation between the phenomenological conception(s) of truth and what religion considers to be its own truth. The present chapter will deal with the first two relations and briefly discuss the particular difficulty the phenomenological method poses to the concept of "religious truth." A full discussion of the topic of truth in religion follows in the next chapter.

In the final chapters of his classic *Religion in Essence and Manifestation* Gerardus Van der Leeuw raises the difficult question: How can there be an *experience* of the transcendent? Is experience not immanent by nature? But if the transcendent does not in some way enter into experience, phenomenology of religion becomes restricted to inner intentions and outer expressions (such as rituals, myths, institutions), while remaining excluded from the intended object of the religious act, namely, a transcendent Absolute. How could a phenomenological analysis ever result in an "essential intuition" *(Wesensschau)* of an object that lies beyond experience? According to Max Scheler, God becomes directly accessible to us only in acts of faith, devotion, and worship. In such acts the believer knows him through an immediate, albeit negative and symbolic, intuition.

"The God of religious consciousness 'is' and lives exclusively in the religious act, not in metaphysical thinking extraneous to religion. . . . The God of religion is the god of the saints and the god of the people, not the cerebral god of the 'intellectuals.' The fount of all religious truth is not scientific utterance but *faith* in the words of the *homo religiosus,* the 'holy man.' "[2]

Only by reflectively retracing the act of faith *from within* does the phenomenologist gain access to its transcendent object. For Scheler, then, a negative *Wesensschau* of what the religious act intends is possible, but only in faith.

Van der Leeuw attempts to solve the problem by distinguishing "religion-as-experience," which is limited to a search for the meaning of life in its totality, from "religion-as-transcendent," exclusively given

---

2. Max Scheler, *On the Eternal in Man,* tr. Bernard Noble (1921, 1954; New York: Harper and Brothers, 1960), p. 134.

in a divine revelation. Phenomenology would be able to deal only with the former while having to abstain from the latter. This answer remains inadequate even by the norms of Van der Leeuw's own practice. His study constantly invokes "revealed" texts. And indeed it should, for without a reflection on what the believer himself regards as the driving motives of his faith — revelation and a divinely granted grace to accept and to live it — phenomenology never comes to grips with the real act. All living religion centers around a nucleus that its believers consider to be transcendently *given*. To exclude that nucleus from phenomenological reflection means to abandon what determines the religious attitude. Van der Leeuw's distinction shows a reluctance, later made into a theological principle by Karl Barth, to subject the core of the Christian faith to the same scrutiny one applies to other religions.

If one thus separates the experience from the revelation that informs it, however, the problems concerning the religious act become insoluble from the start. Must we not assume rather that the experience itself renders its transcendent object, in some way, *intentionally* immanent? To prove that this is possible, a number of philosophers, especially those influenced by Blondel, Rousselot, and Maréchal, have attempted to show that all mental acts are intrinsically related to a transcendent ground of meaning and value. According to their view, all human striving implicitly moves toward an all-transcending end and thus contains a transcendent moment.[3] The question remains, however, whether this transcendent moment can be thematized in a distinct analysis. Those who hold that a transcendent intentionality directs all experience justify such an analysis on the basis that we would not be able to distinguish immanence from transcendence if we could not consider them separately.

Even if we accept the possibility of a transcendent presence within the immanent experience, the question crucial for the phenomenology of religion still stands: whether it can be grasped within the limits that the phenomenological *epochē* sets to the analysis of an intentional act. If it cannot, the phenomenology of religion misses what the believer considers the essence of the religious act. There is no need here to repeat all the ramifications of a problem that I have

---

3. Emerich Coreth, "Transzendenz und Religion," in *Glaube und Säkularisierung,* ed. Julius Morel (Innsbruck: Tyrolia Verlag, 1972), pp. 15-21.

discussed before.[4] But, whatever the final conclusion may be, the religious act certainly displays a distinct quality in the passive attitude that the subject of this act adopts with respect to its object. That object appears as providing its own meaning rather than receiving it from the meaning-giving subject. In the second and the third parts of this essay I shall submit this specific difference to a more critical examination. At this point, it suffices that the religious act *appears* distinct in that its object resists all attempts to define its meaning exclusively as actively projected. However much the religious subject may determine its symbolic expression, the object appears as essentially self-revealing. To focus then on the externally observable devotional actions, congregational structures, and canonical institutions, as if they alone constituted the "phenomena" of religion, without investigating the unique mode in which the subject through them intends a transcendent meaning, would reduce the phenomenology of religion to a classificatory subsection of anthropology and sociology. Precisely the essential transcendence of the object intended by the religious act makes the outward phenomena symbolic *expressions* of what surpasses their ordinary intentionality.

On the other side, the religious act cannot exist without those symbolic expressions. The idea of religion as a purely interior feeling, detachable from its symbolic expression, was first advanced by the young Schleiermacher, who later saw it as a romantic illusion. But that same idea has been revived by a growing number of our contemporaries who no longer find a transcendent meaning in traditional religious symbols and institutions. The phenomenological study of religion resists such as an abstraction: it considers the inner intention indissolubly linked to the outward expression. The phenomenologist considers such external expressions as prayer and sacrifice to be communal activities essential to the religious act. *Because* that act aims at a transcendent (and hence not directly expressible) *telos,* it requires a symbolic representation to exist concretely. Religion consecrates objects in space and time, in order, through them, to transcend the spatial and temporal order itself. It draws its symbols from the entire range

---

4. Louis Dupré, "Husserl's Intentions of Experience," in *A Dubious Heritage: Studies in the Philosophy of Religion after Kant* (New York: Paulist Press, 1977), pp. 75-93. The same problem was discussed in "Philosophy of Religion and Revelation," *International Philosophical Quarterly* 4 (1964): 499-513.

of the finite: inanimate objects, plants, animals, and humans. The very variety of these representations shows how all finite forms fall short of adequately representing a transcendent reality. To compensate for this inadequacy, religious symbolization needs the assistance of the word, the most flexible symbol and the one least bound to a single intentional direction. The *word* alone is capable of linking religious intention to expression. The more spiritually purified a religion is, the more central a function the word will fulfill in its symbolic system. To clarify the specific nature of a religious faith, phenomenology must investigate the symbolic creativity of the human subject in its particularity without losing sight of the essential passivity which that subject experiences at the very heart of this expressive act. Unless he keeps in mind that the religious believer regards his symbols as in some way "revealed," the phenomenologist will miss what the religious believer considers to be essential in faith.

The second part of this essay will draw attention to the difficulty of this task. But first I must return to the question raised by Scheler and Van der Leeuw: Can the phenomenologist truly grasp the meaning of the religious act without actively sharing the believer's faith? Obviously, phenomenological analysis does not coincide with religious belief. One originates in a critical, the other in an accepting attitude. Yet, does the very possibility of understanding the inner meaning of the act not *presuppose* that the critical observer "lives" the act himself? Scheler thought this to be a necessary condition, while Van der Leeuw concluded that the believer's concrete response to what he considers an actual revelation falls beyond phenomenological observation, thus subtracting the entire domain of *concrete* religion from its analysis. In earlier writings I have argued for a qualified version of Scheler's thesis. The phenomenologist must in some way enter into the religious act, either through present or past faith, or also through an actual acquaintance with religious acts and experiences analogous with the ones he attempts to analyze. At any rate, a purely external description, accompanied by *general* theories about religious attitudes and feelings, never yields the kind of intuitive insight that is the goal of phenomenological analysis. From this it follows that the philosopher deprived of empathy with religion is incapable of successfully analyzing its acts, meanings, and symbols. But it also requires, for the phenomenological description of a faith, a substantial acquaintance with its theological self-interpretation. Thus far I have found little that meets those conditions.

II

In this second part, I shall attempt to uncover the unique dialectic between the essential receptivity of the religious act with respect to a transcendent revelation and, on the other side, the active role the believer plays in creating symbols, theories, and norms within which he receives that revelation. An investigation of the self's religious creativity demands a move from phenomenological description to a phenomenological philosophy similar to the one Husserl introduced with his transcendental reduction. Unlike the eidetic reduction, this transcendental one relates the phenomena to a transcendental subject. The transcendental reduction has remained controversial in the phenomenological movement: some, such as Eugen Fink, have strongly asserted its necessity, while others have rejected it as a slide into a transcendental idealism that basically conflicted with Husserl's original project. However one may judge these controversies, a phenomenological study of religion cannot but admit the active part a meaning-giving subject plays in the emergence of institutions, doctrines, and social structures of a particular faith. Religions of the Book (Judaism, Christianity, Islam) derive most of their theoretical and practical norms from what they claim to be a divine revelation contained in canonical Scriptures. But these Scriptures show the personal idiosyncrasies, cultural backgrounds, as well as varying degrees of imaginative and intellectual power of their authors. They borrow their cosmic and social views as well as a good number of their religious conceptions, rituals, and customs from the surrounding culture. These religious representations reflect the cultural outlook of their time and eventually come into conflict with newer cosmologies and different social *mores,* forcing believers to change their interpretation.

On the basis of such active intervention in the religious symbolization, some thinkers have attributed the entire process to human projection. But to do so would be to ignore the awareness of a fundamental passivity that believers maintain in the midst of their symbolic creativity with respect to what they consider to be a transcendent revelation. Even to a believer fully conscious of his active role in the symbolic expression, religion is neither a "projection" as Feuerbach understood it — an attribution of idealized human qualities to an imaginary deity — nor an "illusion" in the Freudian sense of wishes unsupported by reality. The more the believer succeeds in tracing conceptions, structures, and even categories to the constitutive activity of the self, the more the religious act as a whole appears fundamentally given, both in its internal dynamism and in its ultimate object. Unless phenomenology takes account of this irreducible transcendence within the *noema* as well as within the *noesis* of the religious act, the phenomenological reduction misses the specifically religious quality of the act. Indeed, the quality of fundamental givenness that continues to adhere to the act and its object throughout a growing awareness of the subject's own projective power, constitutes the specific difference of the religious act. Nor is this a philosophical or theological a priori: it *appears within* the experience itself. While other cognitive acts *bring* their object to givenness, the religious act, though also elicited by a transcendental ego, intends the irreducible givenness that it encounters both in the impulse and in the directedness of all projective activity.

The phenomenological philosopher who has given the most careful attention to the dialectic of givenness and projection in the religious act is undoubtedly Henry Duméry. For Duméry, as for Husserl, meaning originates under the intentional glance of consciousness and hence must be studied in its relation to a meaning-giving subject. In the religious act, no less than in others, the *ego* constitutes meaning. It projects this meaning over various levels of consciousness: the imaginative, the rational, and the spiritual. The term "projection" in a religious context may easily be misunderstood to refer to a wholly autonomous activity of the mind. In fact, however, projection here refers to the *mediation* by means of which the transcendental subject forms and distributes a *received* impulse within the various psycho-empirical strata of the mind. It transfers the received impulse over the entire field of consciousness.

Consciousness is projective, because it is expressive, because its objective intentionality cannot fail to express itself, to project itself on various levels of representation. This does not mean that these representations themselves become projected upon the objective essence, or upon the reality which this essence constitutes. When contemporary phenomenologists write that the thing itself becomes invested with anthropological predicates and becomes known through those predicates, they merely allude to the need to *represent* the object in order to grasp its intrinsic meaning with all the faculties of the incarnated consciousness. But they do not deny that the object, the objective meaning, the "thing itself," orders, directs, rules the course of these representations.[5]

When Duméry declares consciousness projective, he does not deny that the world with its various geological, biological, and zoological levels possesses a reality of its own, independently of the mind. The world exists as an antepredicative *given* that the mind encounters through the givenness of the body and upon which it then bestows its own intelligibility. The body functions as the unique organ of meaning-giving intentionality that makes the world into a differentiated whole. "The physical object may well have an organized form, but it would remain impenetrable if we had no contact with it through the body."[6]

Similarly, the incarnated mind alone conveys *religious* meaning to a given, preexisting transcendence. All symbols, rites, and religious words have been projected, in the sense here explained, by the human subject. (Obviously, no more than in Kant, is this subject to be identified with the individual self!) Duméry speaks of a "hierogenic" subject that constitutes a sacred sphere by mediating a transcendent impetus with the ordinary life world. In all conscious acts the mind projects meaning over its world: aesthetic, scientific, moral. But the religious meaning differs from all others in that it thematizes the radical receptivity that lies at the ground of all active projection of meaning.

Still, if all religious representations are constituted by a symbol-projecting subject, one may wonder what authorizes the believer to consider the religious act a response to a transcendent revelation. How can he regard its content as truly transcendent, when he knows it to be projected by the mind? The very legitimacy of a philosophy of religion such as Duméry developed (on the basis of Husserl's later

5. Henry Duméry, *La foi n'est pas un cri*, 2nd ed. (Paris: Editions du Seuil, 1959), p. 245 n. Two excellent monographs on Duméry's thought are René F. De Brabander, *Religion and Human Autonomy: Henry Duméry's Philosophy of Christianity* (The Hague: Martinus Nijhoff, 1972); and Henk van Luyk, *Philosophie du fait chrétien. L'analyse critique du christianisme de Henry Duméry* (Paris-Bruges: Desclée de Brouwer, 1964). An anthology of some representative texts of Duméry's writings is *Faith and Reflection*, ed. and intro. Louis Dupré, trans. Stephen McNierney and M. Benedict Murphy (New York: Herder and Herder, 1968).

6. Duméry, *Philosophie de la religion* (Paris: Presses Universitaires de France 1957), 1:105.

writings) depends on the answer to this critical question. Is a transcendent but wholly undetermined impetus sufficient for preserving the concept of a revelation as the believer understands it? Duméry's many critics have answered this question with an unambiguous "no." He himself has attempted to reply to their objections with his theory of the *act-law*. The subject's projective activity obeys a transcendent law that directs its hierophanic creativity. The act-law unites the self to its transcendent source. "The act-law is the ground, or the fine point of personhood, the spark of freedom, the initiative of all determinate creation and all constitution."[7] It corresponds to Plotinus's *intelligible (Nous)* and guides the actual projection of meanings and values. To justify this fundamental passivity at the root of the ego's projective activity, Duméry adds yet another reduction to Husserl's own, to which he refers by a Neoplatonic term, the *henological* (toward "the One" — *to hen*) reduction. While the transcendental reduction refers object to subject, the henological one isolates within the subject itself the Absolute from which that subject draws its projective impulse. In various categories and schemata, the self expresses the relation between itself and this transcendent Absolute from which it derives its creativity. All religious determinations, all divine names, all symbols and representations originate in the hierophanic projection. Yet the projective activity itself is impelled by the presence of the Absolute at the very heart of its creative power.

The particular meaning-intention of the religious act focuses on the *ultimate givenness* of the real in its entirety, including the subject's own projective activity. The individual normally receives this transcendent intentionality from a religious tradition that, in a continuous process of symbolic expression, has built a particular conception of transcendence. Born within the culture based on this tradition, the individual cannot but assume it. Even when repudiating it, he still does so on the basis of principles created by that tradition. Agnostics in the West continue to speak a Judeo-Christian language. But, at the same time, each individual entering a tradition is forced to rethink it and, thereby, inevitably to transform it. Thus, the same religious intentionality never ceases to express itself in new concepts and symbols. Yet each generation of believers regards its religion as essentially identical with that of earlier ones. Nor do believers of diverse levels

7. Duméry, *Philosophie de la religion,* p. 92.

of education find great difficulty in worshiping side by side with each other: at least implicitly they understand that their faith admits of various interpretations.

But it is at the beginning of a religious tradition, and more specifically in the founder(s), that the issue of revelation and projection confronts us with full force. Even here, Duméry insists, the revelatory events are overdetermined by human projection. Founding "facts," historical or legendary, do not become religiously meaningful until they are *interpreted*. Some religions attach a vital significance to the historical quality of those facts. Christianity could not survive as a religion if Jesus had not lived and if the paradigmatic events in his life had never happened. But the fact-Jesus was immediately assumed within a religiously symbolic interpretation that began with Jesus himself. Without symbolic meanings, historical facts could never become objects of religious faith. Many "saw" the events described in the gospel but did not believe because they did not see them as "signs." For the early Christians, the empty tomb and the apparitions gave rise to a faith in Jesus' resurrection and in his divinity. But the observed facts became motives of faith only to those who endowed them with a symbolic "surplus." Others, direct or indirect witnesses of the same facts, refused to believe. To the believer, the ability to "see" is itself transcendently granted as part of a manifestation that appears entirely given. And yet that revealed interpretation itself presupposes a human act of conveying meaning. To deny this does not protect the supernatural quality of the revelation, but it precludes it from being meaningful. The proper task of the phenomenology of religion would then consist in studying the manifestation of transcendence as projected through its interpretive expressions on various levels of consciousness.

Duméry assumes the presence of the Absolute in these projective expressions, but he fails to clarify how exactly that presence determines the projective activity in one sense rather than another. His work reveals both the possibilities and the hazards of a phenomenology of religion conceived, in the spirit of the later Husserl, as a transcendental philosophy. The French philosopher was the first to move his analysis beyond phenomenological description and courageously to address the creative role of the transcendental subject — a role visible to all but recognized by few in the study of religion. Moreover, Duméry has rescued that study from the swampy area of general concepts, allegedly applicable to all religions. Phenomenology needs to investigate the *specific* categories and representations proper to each religion. Finally, he insisted that religion be studied as the believer actually lives it, not as the philosopher decides it ought to be. For Duméry, a critical reflection on living faith is legitimate only as long as the reflection begins by *accepting* the concepts of faith. "Thus the sole duty of the philosopher is to examine the meaning and value that the idea of God bears for living spirituality. He converges on an actually lived intention, without having to take the place of the concrete subject and pursue it himself."[8]

Despite this profession of philosophical modesty, Duméry's work drew an uncommon amount of acrid theological criticism. Theologians vehemently attacked the negative theology of the Absolute that resulted from the henological reduction. An Absolute reduced to utter silence appears incapable of conveying any specific content to revelation. All positive determinations, then, originate in the projective ego, though the hierogenic impulse derives from the One. Such a position, according to its critics, undermines the very idea of revelation as monotheistic Western faith has understood it, namely, as a divine message. Though open to Neoplatonic influences, especially in their mystical theologies, Judaism, Christianity, and Islam have never wavered in asserting that God's aboriginal expression is itself divine. Christians fought their first doctrinal battle to establish that the primal Word is *consubstantialis Patri*. Duméry has no problem with the specificity of a "revelation": he emphatically states that without *particular* religious representations no concrete relation to the Absolute can subsist. The real difficulty lies in the origin and ultimate function of the symbols, laws, and ideas that the believer considers to be revealed. Is their specific character merely defined by cultural needs and aspirations, or is it, as religious believers maintain, an absolute message for all times, cultures, and generations? Duméry, in an attempt to answer the objection of religious relativism, said that "consciousness does not project anything upon the object; it does not cover that object with what does not belong to it. . . . [Consciousness] projects not some of itself upon something other than itself. But [it distributes] the meanings which it intends over diverse levels of expression. Its act is intentional: directed toward the object and attaining it. But it cannot intend it without expressing it at the same time in a

8. Duméry, *Le problème de Dieu* (Paris-Bruges: Desclée de Brouwer, 1957) pp. 33-34; in *Faith and Reflection,* cf. p. 85.

spectrum of various representations."[9] The answer remains ambiguous. Does the Absolute direct the projective act in such a manner that the expression may be considered to be a transcendent message? All depends on the nature of the transcendent impulse — a matter on which Duméry remains exceedingly vague.

Yet this controversy need not detain us, as long as the phenomenological theory of the transcendental ego allows alternatives, and the notion of the Absolute does not exclude self-expression. As for the first condition, if the transcendental ego is the *sole* source of meaning and value, also with respect to the Absolute, the argument is closed: no religion, least of all a religion of revelation, can accept to see its message reduced entirely to a human creation (even if that creation occurs under a transcendent impulse). That the Absolute is intrinsically inexpressible is a Neoplatonic principle that has no ground in Husserl's phenomenology and has from the beginning been rejected by Christian thinkers who unanimously accept the initial statement of the Fourth Gospel — "In the beginning was the Word and the Word was God" — as an incontrovertible principle of their faith. Nor does the separation of absoluteness and expressiveness have any ground in Husserl's phenomenology. Recently, Emmanuel Levinas, following many others in the past, has confirmed that philosophical alternatives to this absolute monism exist.

III

Beside the problems related to transcendence in experience and to the egological reduction, we must still consider how the truth that religion claims for itself may be legitimated within a general theory of truth. In this area, I believe, phenomenology has broken new ground by developing a theory that has proven to be particularly receptive to the religious claim. First, let us briefly survey Husserl's position on the question of truth.

Beginning with the *Logical Investigations,* Husserl claimed that truth consisted in *bringing* the object of cognition to that state of "given"ness which the knower experiences as evident. The subject achieves this

---

9. Duméry, *La foi,* pp. 244-45. The entire section on revelation in that work (*La foi,* pp. 214-25; *Faith and Reflection,* pp. 177-87), was written in answer to critics.

by fulfilling meaning-intentions. Evidence itself, being an *experience,* belongs to a contingent, psycho-empirical order that essentially differs from this ideal meaning-fulfillment. Such an ideal concept of truth contrasts with the traditional one, according to which ideas correspond to reality. Already in the *Logical Investigations,* Husserl had rejected any theory of truth that merely links a mental concept to a "real" state of affairs. The "things themselves" *(die Sachen selbst)* to which his philosophy proclaimed to return, are no less ideal than are the concepts that "conform" to them. "The connection of things, to which the thought-experiences *[Denkerlebnisse]* — the real or the possible — are intentionally related, and, on the other hand, the connection of truths, in which the unity of things *[die sachliche Einheit]* comes to objective validity as that which it is — *both are given together and cannot be separated from each other.*"[10] Clearly, when applied to religion, the requirements of such a theory could never be met by a mere conformity to "facts" — as if a faith would be proven true if the historical data on which it rests were shown to be accurate. Even the alleged facts of a historical religion carry meaning-intentions that, to be true, must be fulfilled in an ideal, interpretive vision. Though facts may crucially matter, as they do, for instance, in the case of Jesus' historical existence, their *meaning* derives from being assumed within a transcendent intentionality. The *possibility* of such an assumption may be justified, but its *necessity* (i.e., that historical facts allow no other interpretation than the one given by the believer) can, I think, never be established in a manner that compels universal agreement.

The exclusion of a naive correspondence theory of truth did not drive Husserl into an epistemology of ideal coherence. That, within a particular *regio* of meaning, intentions remain consistent with one another, does not suffice for them to be true. Religious meanings must be integrated with those of other *regiones.* A coherent system of meaning that conflicts with areas of meaning where evidence has in fact been obtained is not in a position to present credible truth claims. To be sure, the positivist demand that all religious claims be subjected to a verifiability criterion devised for the natural sciences has been

---

10. Husserl, *Logische Untersuchungen* (Halle, 1913), 1:228. I have tried to show that Husserl held an idealist conception of truth from the beginning in "The Concept of Truth in Husserl's *Logical Investigations,*" *Philosophy and Phenomenological Research* 24 (1964): 345-54.

thoroughly discredited. But that does not allow such claims to remain in opposition to fully verified scientific conclusions. Indeed, to remain meaningful at all, religious assertions must submit to a criterion of falsifiability, even though that may be derived from other, more easily accessible areas of meaning.

Yet to define the *specific* nature of religious truth requires more than placing limits around the concept. Husserl's notion of essential intuition *(Wesensschau)* did much to revive the ancient idea of truth as disclosure. The concept of divine illumination that had played a leading role in Western thought from St. Augustine to the sixteenth century, assumed that all truth was reached by a disclosure. It had its roots in Plato, the New Testament, and Augustine. The truth of faith induces a compelling inner evidence that initiates a never-ending search for understanding. In contrast to this theory of illumination, modern philosophy had increasingly emphasized the constitutive role of the subject. Despite his own Kantian connections, Husserl's concept of *Wesensschau* prepared the highly modified version of the older theory that Heidegger and other phenomenologists developed in their notion of truth as disclosure. A process of cognition that results in an intuition of what is essential in the appearances shares a fundamental assumption with the ancient illumination theory, namely, that in truth the real discloses itself — it *appears* with its own evidence. The road to the evidential intuition may be paved by the transcendental subject, but in the final intuition, reality genuinely discloses *itself.* The rational processes that precede the intuition do not constitute its final justification.

Now, religious knowledge ultimately rests on a "revelation," though not always in the restrictive meaning that Jews, Christians, and Moslems attach to the term. It depends on insight in the overall structure of the real *received* from a transcendent source rather than being entirely constituted by the transcendental ego in its encounter with the world. In his unpublished manuscripts Husserl repeatedly refers to an absolute ideal of ethical striving that "far surpasses the transcendental subject."[11] A givenness experienced as "revealed" *ap-*

11. Cf. the manuscripts E III 4 and E III 9 in the Husserl Archives. On Husserl's idea of God, see Stephan Strasser, "Das Gottesproblem in der Spätphilosophie Edmund Husserls," *Philosophisches Jahrbuch* 67, later reprinted in a collection of Strasser's essays, *Bouwstenen voor een filosofische anthropologie* (Hilversum-Antwerp, 1965), pp. 293-311. See also my own, "Husserl's Intentions of Experience," in *A Dubious Heritage,* chap. 4, esp. pp. 80-92.

pears different from a self-induced givenness. Obviously, "disclosure" is the appropriate name for describing the truth of such a "revealed givenness." Religious insight enriches all facets of the real with a new ontological density, with what Gadamer (referring to the nature of symbols) has described as *ein Seinszuwachs,* an increment of Being. This insight appears as given gratuitously, an unearned disclosure of truth. However much the religious mind is aware of its own creative part in concretizing this all-comprehensive vision in rituals, myths, and institutions to express its new symbolic richness, the Source is experienced as surpassing the mind. They serve as privileged symbols allowing the transcendent meaning to penetrate all of reality.

Truth in Religion and
Truth of Religion

If one thing distinguishes traditional religious conceptions of truth from modern philosophical ones, it is the absence, or secondary role, of epistemological concerns. Despite their substantial differences, all religious traditions agree in stressing the ontological and moral qualities of truth over the purely cognitive ones. Truth refers to being, rather than to knowledge. In Sanskrit, the mother tongue of our Indo-European languages, "truth" is *satya* while "being" is *sat*. Gandhi based his lifelong quest for what he called truth upon this identity. In 1932 he formulated it: "Nothing is or exists in reality except Truth. That is why *Sat* or Truth is perhaps the more important name of God. In fact, it is more correct to say that 'Truth is God' than to say that 'God is Truth.'"[1]

The proper attitude with respect to this ontological truth consists in the first place in devotion and fidelity: the path of truth is the path of devotion *(bhakti)* — the only path that leads to God.[2] In a religious vision of this nature lies, I believe, the origin of the so-called correspondence theory, which later became so exclusively cognitive: the

1. Mahatma K. Gandhi, *Yeravda Mandir* in *Gandhi Selected Writings* (New York: Harper, 1972), p. 41.
2. He himself coined a new word based on truth-being to articulate his life project: *satyagraha*. Because *agraha* means firmness, determination, we would understand it as "remaining firmly faithful to the truth of being." For Gandhi truth implies a single-minded devotion to authenticity in speaking, thinking, acting, as well as a willingness to suffer persecution for it. Only after having pursued it morally may we hope that it will reveal itself cognitively. See D. M. Datta, *The Philosophy of Mahatma Gandhi* (Madison: University of Wisconsin Press, 1953), p. 128.

19

consistency between *what* is and one's conduct. Not to be "true" to one's self means, in fact, to descend to a lesser mode of being. Only when we are fully connected with Being shall we be able to *know.* The relation here is exactly the opposite of modern thought, which starts from the primacy of consciousness.[3]

The nature of religious truth consists in the first place in an *ontological* state whereby the relation to God defines the definitive link with Being. That relation also secures access to the source of ultimate meaning. All "true" *knowing* depends on a *being* in the truth. But the transcendent pole of the relation establishes human awareness of the relation as well as the relation itself. Truth in religion implies more than merely admitting that an ontological bond with God exists. The recognition of that bond must itself be given. Truth, then, consists in the right relation to the ultimately real, and only that transcendent reality can enlighten us concerning the nature and even the existence of that relation.

This principle summarizes the fundamental belief about truth not only in the Judeo-Christian tradition but, if I am not mistaken, in all others as well. It marks the constant factor in religious truth. Our own tradition stands out by its increasing emphasis upon the second aspect — the need for a divine disclosure, a revelation. The theology of the Word begins in the first chapter of Genesis and continues right through the New Testament, the Greek and Latin Fathers, medieval Scholasticism and mysticism, Reformed theology, and the Catholic *magisterium.* This tradition announced from the beginning that the Absolute is self-expressive. God speaks essentially and by his very nature. Christianity took this doctrine to its farthest extreme when it proclaimed that God has become Word. In doing so it also declared the reality grounded in God's Being to be expressive. Being as such now becomes self-illuminating, self-manifesting.

In the following pages I shall consider how this religious truth, as conceived *within* the Judeo-Christian tradition, at first developed into the basis and principal analogue of *all* truth. Yet rational reflection

3. "We are so steeped in an epistemological method that we feel compelled to begin with judgment and then introduce 'truth' as a relation to fact to distinguish knowledge from mere belief. But from Gandhi's metaphysical perspective we can within the more general view take account of individual facts as well as individual beliefs and then introduce correspondence as one of the several meanings of truth of judgment" (Paul Grimely Kuntz, "Gandhi's Truth," *International Philosophical Quarterly* 22, 3 [Sept. 1982]: 150).

gradually emancipated this truth from its religious origin until, in the modern age, an independent theory of truth, grounded in the human subject rather than in a divinely established reality, turned into a severe critic *of* religion. In the second part I shall consider both the legitimacy and the limits of a confrontation of religion with a notion of truth that is no longer based upon the transcendent foundation of religion.

Truth in Religion

There exists no single religious view of truth, not even within one religious tradition. Religious typology, always hazardous, is particularly risky in defining a concept as comprehensive, and hence as elusive, as truth. Chances of succeeding in such a task would require an exceptional insight into all major faiths as well as a constant concern not to impose Western categories upon unfamiliar modes of thinking. This discussion will be restricted to some facets of a philosophical reflection, stretching from the Middle Ages to the modern epoch, on a notion of truth of which the New Testament (on a solid biblical foundation) had defined the basic principles. (Elsewhere I have outlined what I consider to be the most significant traits of the New Testament conception of truth as it emerged out of the Hebrew tradition.)

Considering the radicalness with which the New Testament has transformed a terminology borrowed from Hellenistic culture, it appears surprising how early Christian thinkers came to accept the Greek gnosis. Already in the third century, theologians in Alexandria (Clement, Origen) viewed faith itself as the fulfillment of philosophical insight. Yet the new gnosis is not a philosophical rationalization of faith, nor an extension of philosophical understanding: it consists in the self-understanding *of* faith. The gnostic Christian is one who fully *appropriates* what he believes, not one who, besides being Christian, has been educated in philosophy. In insisting that the act of faith contains its own understanding, the Alexandrian and Cappadocian Fathers clearly ruled out the kind of opposition between faith and understanding that lies at the basis of much modern thought.[4]

---

4. See Hans Urs von Balthasar, *The Glory of the Lord: A Theological Aesthetics,* vol. 1, trans. Erasmo Leiva-Merikakis (San Francisco: Ignatius Press; New York: Crossroad, 1982), pp. 137-40.

Initially the Latin West had misgivings not only about mixing worldly wisdom with revealed truth, but even about accepting faith itself as a supreme mode of understanding. Tertullian bluntly opposed one to the other *(credo quia absurdum)*. The great turning point came with Augustine — and not without reservations. He also, after his Neoplatonic period, considered philosophical learning conducive to *impia superbia*.[5] Nonetheless, he judged the search for truth to be *intrinsically* good and salvific. Had Cicero's *Hortentius* not spurred him on toward the quest for eternal wisdom *(Conf.* II, 4)? Though Augustine excepts certain *subjects* from that virtuous search, branding the pursuit of them mere *curiositas,*[6] he attributed a divine, revelatory quality to truth *as such*.

Yet Augustine's major innovation in the conception of religious truth consists in what we may call its interior quality. Whereas originally understanding had come with the faithful acceptance of the gospel, according to Augustine, God teaches each individual soul, though always *in consonance with* the objective testimony of Scripture and ecclesiastical tradition. The divine light that informs the mind, or the interior voice that addresses it, enlightens the believer with regard to not only Scripture but profane learning as well.[7] The very source and condition of truth becomes thereby sacred. With the idea of the interior Master, Augustine achieves a new synthesis between faith and understanding. What for the early Fathers had consisted essentially in a process of explication, now becomes an illumination *simultaneously* derived from different sources (objective and subjective). By subjecting all understanding to a divine illumination that only faith properly identifies, Augustine tightened the original unity of faith and understanding.

With the immanence of divine truth comes the mandate to explore

---

5. *Confessions* V, 3. The reason is eloquently stated in *De vera religione:* "There is no lack of value or benefit in the contemplation of the beauty of the heavens, the arrangement of the stars, the radiant crown of light, the change of day and night, the monthly courses of the moon, the fourfold tempering of the year to match the four elements, the powerful force of seeds from which derive the forms of measure and nature in its kind. But such a consideration must not pander to a vain and passing curiosity, but must be turned into a stairway to the immortal and enduring" (# 52).

6. Not until the high Middle Ages did Western theologians clearly accept *all* knowledge as intrinsically good and destined to find its fulfillment in God.

7. *De magistro,* ## 38-46.

it interiorly, but also the risk of reducing a transcendent message to the conclusion of a process of reason. Augustine always remained aware of both the need for and the limits of a rational exploration. With him the emphasis remains on the *intellectus quaerens fidem,* and faith never ceases to be the ultimately decisive argument. Thus his daring speculations about the Trinity are always accompanied by the spirit of a healthy skepticism about their final success and a cavalier lack of concern concerning their ultimate compatibility.

With Anselm the quest for truth takes a new turn. His "faith seeking understanding," despite its Augustinian tone, moves in a different direction. There is no reason to question his loyalty to St. Augustine, which he explicitly professes in the *Monologium* (preface). Augustine had written: "There are those things that are first believed and afterward understood. Of such a character is that which cannot be understood of divine things except by those who are pure in heart."[8] Anselm echoes: "right order requires that we believe the deep matters of the Christian faith before we presume to discuss them rationally."[9] Yet the very revelation in which we believe urges us to reflect on its implications and to draw its conclusions. One such conclusion consists in the *necessary* character of God's Being. This in turn influences God's relation to his creation (another revealed datum). On the basis of these data Anselm develops a logic of immanence and transcendence that encompasses even the historical event of Christ's incarnation. Inasmuch as God is necessary in his very Being, divine redemptive activity must also result from an inner necessity.

Yet, in deducing the inner necessity of God's dealings with the historical contingencies resulting from human decisions, Anselm in fact goes well beyond the data of revelation. Thus he reduces God's choice after the fall to the following: "To deal rightly with sin without satisfaction is to punish it. Not to punish it is to remit it irregularly." In attributing the need for satisfaction to divine nature itself, Anselm makes such fundamental assumptions concerning divine freedom — neither stated nor implied in the revealed text — that his theory can no longer be called an explication of that text. Indeed, it contains the

8. *De diversis quaestionibus,* 83, 48.
9. *Cur Deus Homo?* trans. Jasper Hopkins and Herbert Richardson, in *Anselm of Canterbury,* bk. 1, chap. 2 (Toronto: Edwin Mellen Press, 1976).

seeds of all future religious rationalism. It certainly surpasses what revelation assisted by reason enables one to say about God's disposition to the world. Anselm obviously feels the need to give a more complete account of the relations between God and creation. Thus a project proclaimed to be based on the *data revelationis,* and preceded by an unambiguous profession of faith, changed its nature in the course of its execution.[10]

Still, Anselm's rationality remains throughout a devout rationality, illumined by a monastic vision, that never consciously deviates from the principle stated in the *Proslogion: Quaero credere ut intelligam, non autem intelligere ut credam.* Faith remains the basic presupposition of all genuine understanding. Yet a trend was set and the rationalism that emerged with Abelard was far less pious. No theological knowledge of Scripture was needed, he thought, to investigate the truth of religious mysteries. Logic alone sufficed to understand even such recondite dogmas as the Eucharist or the Trinity. The reception of Aristotle's systematic works made the study of theology itself something it had never been before — namely, a *science* in the Aristotelian sense. With it came the epistemic distinction between two orders of knowledge: a philosophical and a theological.

In the very beginning of the *Summa Theologiae* (Article 2), Thomas Aquinas raises the question: Is sacred doctrine a science? Of particular interest is the purely Aristotelian definition by which he supports his affirmative answer — namely, that "science" progresses from self-evident principles. Principles "known by the natural light of reason" appear on an even footing with principles "established by the light of a higher science, namely, the science of God and the blessed." To us such an equation may appear surprising, for it proves by means of what has to be proven. Need not the so-called science of God and the blessed itself be first established as a science? But Thomas takes for granted the epistemic solidity of the manner in which we gather the "first principles" of sacred doctrine. A little later he fully admits that they are *articuli fidei* (articles of faith), hence direct objects of revelation. "As other sciences do not argue in proof of their principles but argue from their principles to demonstrate other truths in these sciences, so

10. On the ambivalence of Anselm's attitude, see William Collinge, "Monastic Life as a Context for Religious Understanding in St. Anselm," *American Benedictine Review* 35, 4 (1984): 378-88.

this doctrine does not argue in proof of its principles, which are the articles of faith, but from them it goes on to prove something else."[11] The higher "science" then turns out to be revelation — an interpretation of his text that Aristotle would have found surprising. Because Thomas is concerned only about the formal procedure from principles (however certified) to conclusions, he unhesitatingly transplants the method from one to the other.

Such a scientific definition of religious truth differed too obviously from the one advocated by Augustine and the entire Greek Christian tradition that preceded him to remain unchallenged. The Paris condemnations of 1277 as well as the nominalist development in theology profoundly shook it. Still, in the end, Thomas's "scientific" presentation of religious truth may not be as far removed from the Augustinian tradition as it seems. In themselves the articles of faith are only "external" principles: to be convincing at all they must be accompanied by an "interior light that induces the mind to assent." The principles themselves function like sense data, which do not become intelligible until the mind illumines them. The light of faith provides the formal element that converts the objective data of faith into religious truth.[12] For Aquinas as for Augustine what ultimately determines the act of faith is God's own internal witness. The truth about God can come only from God, and in faith human beings respond to God's self-witness. Aquinas moves within a well-established tradition initiated by the Fourth Gospel: religious truth derives its constitutive evidence from a divine illumination. The external object of belief (the "principles") reveals itself as *true* only within the act of faith.

Nominalism soon undid the synthesis of faith and reason that Thomas and his followers had achieved. Religious truth, though still possessing the intrinsic evidence of experience, could no longer count on the concomitant support of reason. Henceforth, there would be two separate conceptions of truth: the one of reason based on the presumed harmony between mind and nature, the one of theology

---

11. *Summa Theologiae*, I, q. 1, a. 8.

12. "For Thomas, neither Christian doctrine nor the miracles that attest to it would say anything to man without the *interior instinctus et attractus doctrinae (In John,* c. 6, i. 4, n. 7; c. 15, i. 5, n. 5; *In Rom.* c. 8, i. 6), which he also calls *inspiratio interna* and *experimentum*" (Hans Urs von Balthasar, *The Glory of the Lord,* 1:162.

resting on an authority beyond nature. The *truth of religion,* as established by philosophy, became distinct from faith's own truth. Philosophy's first task consisted in proving the existence of God by purely rational arguments. Of course, Anselm and already Augustine had construed some rational formulation of the mind's ascent to God. But medieval writers had never intended to do so independently of the religious sources (including revelation) that had provided the idea of God in the first place. They wanted to show that this idea, far from conflicting with reason, fully agreed with that of an infinite Being that they considered to be necessary for supporting the finite.

In the modern age the purport of the arguments was to prove, independently of any intrinsically religious evidence, the existence of a particular being called God. The "truth" of religion must hereby emerge from a process of reasoning from the finite to the necessity of an infinite principle. Even if the proof succeeds in establishing the independent existence of such a principle *beyond* the world — a most difficult task indeed — it still has to establish that this principle coincides with the God of religion. Aquinas, Maimonides, or Avicenna did not face such excessive challenges, for they started by accepting the God of faith, and then proceeded to show that to do so is not irrational. Once the finite's need of the infinite was established, they did not hesitate to identify this infinite with their religious idea of God: from theological reflection they knew already that, among other things, the God in whom they believed must be infinite and necessary. This procedure often leads to careless thinking, however. Because the authors knew the outcome beforehand, they were anxious to reach the goal and have it all over with. But in principle the method is unobjectionable.

In contrast with this method, arguments that by a process of sheer reasoning pretend to arrive at full-fledged religious conclusions assume that the phenomenal world is capable of yielding sufficient information about the nature of what transcends it. To conclude to a transcendent ground, or to postulate such a ground in order to make the real intelligible, is not yet to attain the idea of God as religious faiths have traditionally conceived it. Is the absolutely intelligible — which many philosophers require to found the intelligibility of the real — the perfect Being intended by the religious act? Karl Jaspers's philosophy of transcendence is there to prove that one does not necessarily imply the other: the philosophical idea of transcendence, though it invites further investigation, leads by itself to no specific religious content. Only from a religious confrontation with the divine in "revelation" and "grace" can transcendence receive such a content. An autonomous study of Being or consciousness can state the problem; it cannot provide the answer.

In the arguments for the existence of God, modern thought reveals most clearly its attitude with respect to religious truth. It assumes that there is no specifically *religious* truth. Religion has been allotted a field of consciousness ruled by methods of its own, but the final judgment on truth has been withdrawn from its jurisdiction and removed to the general domain of epistemic criteriology. Revelation may "add" to what we "know" by natural means, but it remains subject to the general rules of truth and credibility. These rules did not originate in religion's native land: they are a creation of the modern mind, a mind unwilling to have the criteria of truth established by any source outside itself. *Truth,* if still granted to religious assertions, no longer springs from within faith but is extrinsically conveyed to faith. In the traditional view religious truth originated in some sort of participation in the revealed mystery of divine Being. The human subject, now the source of truth, was then no more than a receptacle endowed with a divine potential for apprehending the truth as divinely revealed. With this separation from faith, and perhaps as a cause of it, goes a gradual separation of experience from faith. In early centuries, faith, far from being opposed to experiential evidence, was never considered to be complete without it; later it came to occupy an order of its own with a minimum of experiential content. Experience became the privilege of a spiritual elite — the so-called "mystics."

Truth of Religion

If religion by its own account provides the basis of its own truth, can we move to a basis outside the domain of faith and yet hope to evaluate that truth fairly? Can faith accept any judgment critical of its truth that originates in an autonomous philosophy independently of the principles of faith itself? Can any statement be made about the truth *of* religion that does not coincide with the truth *in* religion itself? This much seems certain: a critical examination that on the basis of pure reason, independently of the religious experience proper, attempts to establish or disestablish "the truth of religion" must indeed result in distortion. Because modern philosophical theories of truth were developed for the purpose of securing a foundation for scientific practice, their principles may appear unfit for evaluating the specific nature of religious truth. Yet such a conclusion would be premature and, I hope to show, in the end unjustified. The basic models of truth used in those theories predate the scientific concerns of the modern age. They may, in fact, have grown out of a religious soil. Such was almost certainly the case with the disclosure model. But truth as correspondence and truth as coherence were also formulated well before their modern, critical formulations. Clearly, philosophy has developed these ancient models of truth on the basis of careful (albeit often unduly limited) analyses of the cognitive act. To compare religious claims to those models by no means commits one to the antitheological assumptions that often accompany their appearance in modern philosophy. But neither do we propose to "justify" religious truth in the light of that philosophy. Unless one assumes the basic legitimacy of the religious act on its own merits, attempts at an all-comprehensive justification inevitably fail. Truth, as Spinoza taught, must prove itself: one cannot prove it to be true by another "truth" that presumably stands outside it.

The following argument presupposes the existence of a truth proper to religion. In comparing it with the existing models of truth I merely intend to investigate the aptitude of these models for clarifying that religious *fact*. In a sense, then, what is being examined here is philosophy — or at least its available apparatus — rather than religion. To be sure, if the concept of religious truth proved to be radically incompatible with any of the existing models, the critical believer would have serious grounds for questioning the "truth of religion." For truth, in whatever manner envisaged, must, in principle, be able to adjudicate all legitimate claims of truth. If recent philosophy has often rejected the legitimacy of religious claims, the *application* of the basic models, rather than the models themselves, may be at fault. If, however, the religious concept of truth were to prove intractably resistant to *any integration* with other concepts of truth (such as the scientific ones) within the existing models, this would create a serious problem for the truth-claims inherent in religion. All the more so since these models originated long before any positivist restrictions were attached to them.

Religion unfolds its own truth, yet it is forced to do so within the available categories of general discourse. Revelation itself cannot be rendered intelligible unless it still proves capable of being assumed within the established patterns of speaking and thinking. However sublime and unique a message may be, in order to be expressed, it must adopt an *existing* language and thereby integrate itself within a *praxis* of discourse.

Religious Truth as Correspondence

The correspondence between word and reality appears even in the earliest tradition, if not as the central core of religious truth, at least as one of its essential components. Truth, including religious truth, requires that our words or concepts conform to things as they are in themselves. Philosophy, after it took the critical epistemic turn, found nothing but insoluble problems in such a neat division between a purely "mental" concept and a purely "real" object. Precisely the invincible difficulties inherent in the unproven assumption of a harmony between the mind and the world led to Kant's radical reversal of the correspondence theory.

After his "Copernican revolution" the line that distinguishes the correspondence from the coherence theory becomes hard to draw. In the previous chapter I mentioned that Husserl's famous "things themselves" proved to be as ideal as the concepts that related to them. The relation between the mind and its intentional object came to be interpreted as one of immanent objectivity. The intuition of truth in the end, then, is the outcome of a process in which we bring the object to givenness. A thing is *given* when it is brought to ideal presence. Clearly, in such an immanent interpretation the distinction between a theory of correspondence and one of coherence approaches the vanishing point.

Even without following the Kantian reinterpretation to its idealist extremes, we cannot but regard the appeal to "the facts," which some contemporary critiques of religion continue to make, as patently uncritical. No facts are perceivable without a screen of interpretation that converts data into objects or facts. To perceive a complex of data as a fact always includes seeing it through an interpretation. In the case of religion, which deals with the ultimate structure of the real itself, interpretation plays a particularly significant and inevitably controversial part. It is quite common for two persons confronted with the same state of affairs to see it as religious or as nonreligious, and to do so without in the least contradicting each other on the relevant observable data. Both may agree on the basic interpretation, but one may feel the need for a further justification, which the other rejects or considers unnecessary. On a practical and on an ordinary theoretical level, believers and unbelievers interpret the world in a manner so similar that they may intimately collaborate with one another on social or scientific projects without ever encountering major differences of interpretation. Basic, partial interpretations suffice for practical, scientific work, and even for a general cultural exchange. Nevertheless, to those who hold them, religious interpretations shed a different light on all aspects of the real, and on a deeper level they affect their emotional, ethical, and motivational attitudes.

A philosophical evaluation of the "truth of religion" on the basis of a correspondence theory of truth, then, requires taking into account not only the legitimacy of separate levels of interpretation but, in addition, possible conflicts of interpretation made on one level with those made on other levels. Still religious truth must submit to the rules of correspondence. For truth in religion claims to correspond to what ultimately *is,* and proclaims to be a conversion, both moral and ontological, toward Being, contrary to appearance and deception. The possible discrepancy between one and the other, as well as the process required to reach the state of total correspondence, suggests the existence of a separation between the mind and the ultimate reality that religious truth claims to bridge. Moreover, the "truth" thus attained is presented as *revealed* — that is, *given* to the mind from a principle or level of being that surpasses the mind's own reality. The *process* of truth overcomes an initial duality between the mind and the "inner word" of revelation.

Religious Truth as Coherence

Today most truth theories, implicitly or explicitly, refer to coherence. This is particularly the case with religious truth. Many who had become disheartened about the prospect of religious truth meeting the demands for empirical verification advanced by positivists and empiricists saw in the newly formulated coherence theory an escape from their troubles. Linguistic theories, such as that found in Wittgenstein's *Philosophical Investigations,* would legitimate any discourse, independently of others, provided the discourse would consistently apply the rules it set itself. Undoubtedly the coherence theory has protected the realm of religious meaning against undue intrusions of other realms. Each particular system, each "significant whole" as Harold Joachim defined it in his classical *The Nature of Truth,* obeys laws of its own that differ from those of other significant wholes.[13] An internal articulation organically integrates the separate elements into a unity of meaning. In the case of religion such a recognition of a relative autonomy becomes particularly important, for it exempts us from having to apply the same criteria that condition purely objective knowledge.

Yet the theory requires several qualifications if it is to apply to religious discourse. Coherence easily turns into closedness. To make genuine truth-claims, a system must be coherent not only within itself but also with other systems. This requires at the very least that principles inherent in what may be called "basic" interpretations of experience do not contradict those implicit in a "higher" or more remote system of interpretation, where religious truth places its stake. Recent debates on religious truth tend to neglect this point. To show that the discourses of religion and of physics substantially differ is not sufficient to exclude a priori any possible conflict.

That religion has staked out its own realm of discourse does not dispense it from having to enter into dialogue with other realms and to render its claims compatible with the "basic" interpretations of common sense and the physical sciences. Even the principles of falsifiability and verifiability that rule these interpretations should not be immediately dismissed as not applying to this "higher" realm. In withdrawing religious truth from universal criteria of meaning, we rescue it from outside criticism only to drown it in total meaninglessness.

If truth in religion were not to share some basic assumptions with other areas of truth, the term "truth" as we understand it today would

13. Oxford: Clarendon Press (1906), 1969, p. 68. The importance of Joachim's expression lies in its distinguishing "the determining characteristics of the 'significant whole'" from a logical nexus that secures a certain cohesion of various elements without intrinsically relating them.

cease to preserve any meaning at all. Religious truth, while being distinct, nevertheless relates to all aspects of life. A philosophical theory of truth tolerates neither unmediated pluralism nor epistemic relativism, since one system of truth cannot remain totally unrelated to another.[14] Closing religious doctrines off from other realms of thought may in the end create worse problems than open conflicts with them. Precisely the failure to harmonize those doctrines with the scientific worldview has rendered religion so improbable to many of our educated contemporaries as not to deserve any serious consideration. C. C. Broad, while agreeing with the claim that nothing in modern science "refutes" the belief in miracles and in an afterlife, nevertheless dismissed it for being totally out of tune with the scientific world picture: "there is literally nothing but a few pinches of philosophical fluff to be put in the opposite scale to this vast coherent mass of ascertained facts."[15] A preposterous conclusion, to be sure — but one made possible by the increasing "hermetization" of religious discourse.

To avoid the problems of modern culture, believers tend to compartmentalize their worldview. Facing social, psychological, and scientific developments that they feel unable to integrate with their faith, they disconnect their unexamined religious beliefs from the rest of their convictions, as an island of truth isolated from the mainland of modern culture. Yet the believer should know that these convictions on a basic level draw a line of probability beyond which even the most hallowed "revelation" becomes rationally inadmissible. Rather than outrightly rejecting the validity of the principle of falsifiability in religious truth, believers should question the one-sided manner in which the positivist usually applies it. They may rightly refuse to accept criteria that fail to account for the specific quality of religious beliefs. But they should at least admit the fact, supported by daily

14. In the words of William Christian: "If there are domains of truth, then philosophers, taken collectively, would have the following complex project, among others, on their hands. They would be responsible for (1) formulating principles of judgment in various domains of discourse, (2) formulating general conditions of truth and showing how truth conditions in various domains specify the general conditions, and (3) exploring patterns of relatedness among different domains" (William A. Christian, "Domains of Truth," *American Philosophical Quarterly*, 12 [1975]: 62).

15. C. D. Broad, *Philosophy and Psychical Research* (London: Routledge, Kegan Paul, 1953), p. 235.

apostasies, that faith is in principle falsifiable and that the limits of probability, however different from one person to another, cannot be stretched indefinitely.

Taken by itself the theory of coherence proves insufficient to account for the most strongly held claim of religious truth — namely, that it originates *outside* of the system. The case of structuralism should illustrate the limits of the coherence theory. A consistent structuralist system, if I understand it correctly, tolerates no intrusion from beyond, indeed, no genuine novelty. Since the context alone must account for any possible appearance, the form of new phenomena was a priori implied in the structure itself. Not to admit genuine difference is, of course, fatal to any idea of religious truth which implies a transcendent revelation. Precisely because Derrida perceived the inability of a closed structuralism to admit genuine novelty, he developed a theory of language that would allow him to move beyond intrinsic socio-linguistic limitations. His philosophy of the creative *word* breaking through the given, whereby the signifier transcends the signified, appears, paradoxically, to reopen the way to religious transcendence.[16]

Having expressed these objections against the potential of the coherence theory to serve as exclusive model for a philosophical evaluation of religious truth, I nevertheless admit its unique appropriateness for legitimating the *relative* autonomy and distinct identity of religious discourse. But by itself alone the theory of coherence cannot do justice to the characteristic truth of such a discourse.

Disclosure

The correspondence and coherence models remain indispensable for understanding the truth of religion. But with the subjective turn of modern thought they became removed from what religion itself has traditionally understood to be the essence of its truth. What remains of the truth of revelation in theories for which the criterion of equation

16. How little this effect is intended, however, appears in the fact that the creative power is restricted to the human being — the sole maker of words. Derrida himself supports his position in a passage that could have been written by an Italian humanist: "Consciously or not, the idea that man has of his aesthetic power corresponds to the idea he has about the creation of the world and to the solution he gives to the radical origin of things" (*Writing and Difference* [University of Chicago Press, 1978], p. 10).

or of coherence is the human subject? The disclosure theory appears less tainted by modern subjectivism and therefore better suited to recognize the specific nature of *religious* truth.

In recent discussions that theory has moved once again to the front stage of the philosophical scene. But its origins lie hidden in the beginnings of Western thought. We find it in Plato and Plotinus, of course, but, before them, already in Parmenides' famous poem and, even earlier, in the dark recesses of Greek myth. In its modern form it reasserts the priority of *ontological* over epistemic truth. "Truth," Heidegger states, does not possess its original seat in the proposition but in a disclosure "through which an openness essentially unfolds."[17] Allowing things to be, to disclose themselves in the open, is the very essence of freedom. Though the essence of truth lies in freedom, its focus is not on the subject, but on the openness within which Being itself appears.

Such a theory definitely appears more hospitable to religious truth. Indeed, its origin is clearly religious. But here the problem meets us from the opposite angle. How will a theory so obviously dependent upon the traditional idea of illumination meet the modern critical demand that truth *justify* itself? *Disclosure* may be the concept in which religion views its own truth, but will philosophy accept it as the truth *of* religion?

Since the days of Heidegger and Marcel hermeneutic philosophy has gone a long way in attempting to justify the disclosure theory, not, to be sure, by means of the critical method (which would soon reduce disclosure to a subjective source), but by a careful analysis of modes of cognition that illuminate Being without being restricted by the epistemic criteria of the positive sciences. Thus, both aesthetic and historical consciousness attain truth in a manner that surpasses the demands of truth as equation, namely, historical accuracy and aesthetic "imitation of nature." Obviously, the critical norms used in establishing the foundations of the positive sciences do not apply here.

Gadamer clearly defined the issue: "Our task demands that we recognize in it an experience of truth which must not only be critically justified, but which itself is a mode of philosophizing."[18] "Critical"

---

17. "On the Essence of Truth," trans. John Sallis, in *Basic Writings,* ed. David F. Krell (New York: Harper & Row, 1976), pp. 129-33.

18. *Wahrheit und Methode* (Tübingen: J. C. B. Mohr, 2nd ed., 1965), p. xxxv.

justification (the term itself is misleading in this context!) here consists in a particular "mode of philosophizing," a retracing in *actu reflecto* of what we are actually doing in *actu exercito,* rather than in establishing the kind of critical foundation that philosophy provides for the sciences. The purpose of this immanent reflection is to uncover the light it sheds on Being and on human existence within Being. The real test of disclosure consists in establishing its ontological significance. This, according to Gadamer (in the third part of *Truth and Method*), occurs in a fundamental reflection on language.

In his discussion of the image, Gadamer refers to the ontological quality of the iconic symbol by the term *Seinszuwachs* — augmentation of Being. The term eminently applies to the truth disclosed in religious symbols, particularly in religious language. Precisely in this ontological nature of religious disclosure resides its characteristic truth. This, I believe, is ultimately what Hegel had in mind when he declared the Christian religion to be essentially "true" — that is, expressing the deepest dimension of Being: "[Christian doctrine] is not merely something subjective but is also an absolute, objective content that is in and for itself, and has the characteristic of truth."[19] Rather than submitting this disclosure to antecedent philosophical criteria, Hegel considers philosophy itself dependent on what he considers the prior, religious disclosure: "[the standpoint of religion] is the affirmation that the truth with which consciousness is actively related *embraces all content within itself.* Hence this relation of this consciousness to this truth is itself the highest level of consciousness, its absolute standpoint."[20] The absoluteness of religious truth lies in the fact that its disclosure includes all reality without having to refer to any reality outside of itself, and that it implies its own necessity.[21]

But then Hegel adds that the truth of religion is fully disclosed only when religion itself reinterprets its representational form through philosophy. The *justification* of religious truth — which formerly had mostly consisted in the critical *reflection upon* an already established truth — now constitutes *itself* as truth. Hence the disclosure of reli-

19. *Vorlesungen über die Philosophie der Religion.* Part 1, *Der Begriff der Religion,* ed. Walter Jaeschke (Hamburg, 1981), p. 25 (*Lectures on the Philosophy of Religion.* Part 1, *The Concept of Religion,* ed. Peter C. Hodgson [Berkeley: University of California Press, 1984], p. 106).

20. *Vorlesungen,* p. 219; *Lectures,* part 1, p. 315.

21. *Vorlesungen,* p. 223; *Lectures,* part 1, p. 319.

gious truth is not completed *within faith* itself. At this point we may wonder whether Hegel is not withdrawing with one hand what he had given with the other. Still Hegel consistently claims ontological ultimacy for religious disclosure, asserting that it contains an onto-logical richness unparalleled by any other mode of truth.

Theologians and many philosophers were quick in appropriating the disclosure theory for their explanation of religious truth. They felt that they were merely returning the concept of truth to its place of origin. Of course, philosophers still found themselves stranded with the arduous task of *justifying* this ontological manifestation without appealing directly to a supernatural revelation. Many chose to ignore this difficult issue and were satisfied with *describing* the unique disclo-sure that takes place in the religious act. One need not decide on the natural or supernatural origin, they felt, in order to see in the religious act an illumination within which all previous contents and relations come to stand in a new light. Even as we suddenly perceive a picture that, without any change in the configuration, totally transforms a mere complex of lines and colors, so a religious disclosure conveys to ordinary reality a symbolic and metaphorical quality.

But how does the ontological disclosure justify the specific beliefs and rules that provided the occasion for it? I have already indicated how the traditional requirements of verification and falsification in a general way also apply to religion. For the religious believer, the ontological disclosure occurs entirely *within* the language of revelation. In the Christian revelation, God's living Word provides, with its own disclosure, the conditions for the internal justification of its truth. The Spirit given with, and in, the Word testifies to the veracity of the message and enables the believer to see its evidence. But such a description is not likely to satisfy the philosopher. The idea of a divine revelation, far from providing the justifying evidence that disclosure requires, stands itself in dire need of support. Nor should we assume, as Gadamer does (in analogy with the way revelation justifies itself to the believing mind), that language justifies its own disclosure. For the disclosure of language by itself provides no adequate criteria for dis-tinguishing truth from falsehood — an essential task in the traditional justification of truth.

It is, of course, true that *to the believer* the disclosure granted through revelation justifies itself. But this is not the case for the non-believer. Religious disclosure, then, does not appear to possess the kind of impartial, universally accessible quality which philosophy demands in truth. It requires an involved participation, a personal commitment rather than detached intellectual insights. For this reason the phenomenologists Gerardus van der Leeuw and Max Scheler concluded that the religious act and its intentional object cannot be understood unless one shares the faith that conditions them — that is, unless one accepts the transcendence of its object.[22] Clearly, if this implies the need to convert philosophy into faith, philosophy would *eo ipso* cease to justify the religious disclosure altogether. Yet according to another, milder interpretation, an adequate philosophical evaluation of religious disclosure would require only that the critic be *in some way* directly acquainted with its experience. This acquaintance need not consist in a full participation in the faith on which one reflects: it may be no more than the memory of an actual faith, or even no specific faith at all, but only a general religious sensitivity. Even so, the restriction prevents philosophical reflection on the religious disclosure from being universally accessible. But can "truth" that cannot justify itself on a universal basis still be considered philosophically justifiable?

Before answering this question negatively, we should realize that the aesthetic experience falls under the same restrictions. Only a person actually acquainted with such an experience qualifies for passing philosophical judgment on it. Rather than claiming that there is no truth in the disclosure of art and religion, one should conclude that the truth of disclosure, aesthetic or religious, intrinsically differs from scientific or historical truth, even though they may share *some* rules. But this much remains certain: religion introduces its own truth without allowing itself to be measured *definitively* by any extrinsic or universal norm.

Recently some theologians have attempted to justify the theory of religious disclosure on the basis of Heidegger's existential interpretation. Thus Rudolf Bultmann has interpreted the Christian revelation as disclosing a new dimension in existence. But granted that that would constitute a philosophical justification of its claim to truth (which many would deny), it still fails to recognize the unique nature of the *religious* disclosure in assuming that a transcendent revelation

---

22. Gerardus van der Leeuw, *Religion in Essence and Manifestation* (New York: Harper, 1960), p. 61. See my own evaluation in *A Dubious Heritage* (New York: Paulist Press, 1977), pp. 76-79.

can be exhaustively translated into existential terms. Kierkegaard, with his own intense interest in an existential realization of the gospel, remained acutely aware of the ultimate incongruity between transcendent meaning and immanent existence, and therefore considered all genuinely religious truth to remain permanently hidden from direct communication. Religious truth is, indeed, interiorly disclosed, but never directly. It remains, as Kierkegaard put it, a "pathetic-dialectical" message — that is, one that after having been passively received must still be dialectically interiorized. This translation into existence, essential to the religious disclosure, consists in a never-ending process of mediation.

The self-manifestation of the transcendent is, in the end, neither self-understanding nor understanding of Being. Though contributing to both, it also surpasses them in referring to the inexpressible. Mystical writers have fully accepted this paradox. John of the Cross introduces a discussion of "naked truths" with the disconcerting preface: "You should know, beloved reader, that what they in themselves are for the soul is beyond words."[23] He then proceeds by declaring the knowledge of God a subject on which "in no way anything can be said."[24] Nor is this inexpressible knowledge "manifest and clear"; rather it is "sublime" because it is "transcending what is naturally attainable."[25] These paradoxes of mystical knowledge affect religious truth as such: it discloses the presence of a reality that can never be disclosed itself. Without accounting for the unique case of religion, a philosophical theory of truth-as-disclosure, far from "justifying" religious truth, remains incapable of understanding it.

Religious disclosure is truth that, in its essentials, refuses to submit to external criteria. To see this conclusion confirmed one need only reflect on the notion of *experience* as religion uses it. Any disclosure takes place in some mode of what we vaguely refer to as experience. If experience means no more than the various mental processes by which persons, actively and passively, respond to the stimuli of their life world, then it bears no relation to truth. Yet if, as Aristotle taught,[26]

---

23. *Ascent of Mount Carmel,* trans. Allison Peers (Garden City, N.Y.: Doubleday-Image, 1958), II, 26, 1.
24. *Ascent of Mount Carmel,* II, 26, 5.
25. *Ascent of Mount Carmel,* II, 26, 8.
26. *Analytica Posteriora* B 19.

experience yields a unique form of insight that, though not scientific, nevertheless attains a kind of cumulative and never completed universality, then it is at least on the way to truth. Experience defines its own meaning: those who experience learn in the process itself *what* they are experiencing. This insight cannot claim the title of truth, however, until, beyond a mere empirical awareness, it attains some form of ideal necessity and thereby discloses a permanent feature of the real as such. Yet the truth of experience does not lie exclusively in the knowledge for which it establishes the precondition, but also, and primarily as Gadamer points out, in the process itself.[27] Precisely in following the very course of consciousness in time, experience acquires its unique purchase on truth — namely, that it is and becomes increasingly *my own* experience. It hereby endows truth, on whichever level acquired, with some kind of *practical indubitability* that, though not warranting freedom from error, nevertheless secures incontrovertible evidence.

Religious disclosure occurs *within* a highly personal or intensely communal experience and, even when raised to the level of universal truth, retains this personal or communal quality in being a *truth-for-me* or a *truth-for-us*. Revelation discloses more about the believer than about God: in it a transcendent message interacts with an immanent experience. This tight link between the message and the experience does not render religious disclosure a purely subjective affair. The reality that we experience — in this case, the transcendent reality as communicated in revelation — defines the nature of the experience and endows it with its own authority — not the other way around.[28]

This, however, by no means implies that in the immanence of one's experience the believer gains direct access to the transcendent object received by it. God never *appears* in the manner in which a sense object bodily presents itself.[29] Nonetheless, faith carries an evidence of its own that, without the manifest presence of its object, illuminates the believer's relation to it as vital to the understanding of

27. *Wahrheit und Methode,* pp. 333-37.

28. Edward Schillebeeckx, *Christ: The Experience of Jesus as Lord,* trans. John Bowden (New York: Crossroad, 1981), p. 37.

29. I leave the complex case of the mystical vision out of consideration. Besides being highly exceptional, the precise nature of visions and locutions remains obscure even by the mystics' own accounts. They could hardly be more than expressions of a more intense but *still mysterious* experience of presence.

him- or herself and of all reality. The experience of revelation draws the *decisive* arguments for verifying its content not from external sources but from itself. Believers assume that what they know of the divine object they know through that object itself. Christians have traditionally expressed this in the doctrine of the indwelling Spirit who teaches them "the entire faith." Eckhart echoed it in his word that the eye with which we see God is the eye with which God sees God. Clearly this kind of evidence provides no scientific support for its truth, nor does it increase our theoretical knowledge of the world. But it opens up a different *perspective* on metaphysical insight as well as on empirical investigation, and brings with it a unique yet highly personal justification of its own truth.

Philosophy and
the Mystery of Evil

The Concrete-Religious Versus
the Rationalist-Abstract Approach

Theodicy today enjoys the dubious reputation of a failed experiment.
Few outside the small circle of persistent believers in it would grant
that it has succeeded in accomplishing what it set out to do. That
failure has become more painfully apparent as our sensitivity to, as
well as the increased visibility of, evil, both moral and physical, have
intensified our questioning. The sheer magnitude of evil that our age
has witnessed in death camps, nuclear warfare, and internecine tribal
or racial conflicts has lowered our tolerance level for what once was
accepted as a necessary part of life. Indeed, the presence of evil has
impressed itself more powerfully than has the presence of God upon
the minds of many of our contemporaries. For them the primary
question is no longer how God can tolerate so much evil, but rather
how the more tangible reality of evil still allows the possibility of God's
existence. Beyond religious and ideological differences our contemporaries have attained a remarkable agreement that evil "was not
meant to be," that it constitutes an alien invasion into our lives. To
an unprecedented degree we feel the need to "justify" the presence
of evil in our world. Yet we have lowered or abandoned our expectations to receive an adequate answer to the question *Unde malum?*
from philosophy. Indeed, speculative attempts to reduce the question
to a theoretical issue tend to render the reality of evil less rather than
more acceptable.

41

Evil invites philosophical speculation, yet it is the cliff on which philosophy suffers shipwreck. By a paradox unique to our time we remain simultaneously aware of both terms of the opposition. Schopenhauer anticipated the paradox when he wrote: "Without doubt it is the knowledge of death, and along with this the consideration of the suffering and misery of life, which gives the strongest impulse to philosophical reflection and metaphysical explanation of the world. If our life were endless and painless, it would perhaps occur to no one to ask why the world exists, and is just this kind of world it is."[1] Two distinct philosophical reactions have emerged. Some contemporary thinkers attempt to repair by one philosophy the damage wrought by another, believing that what has been philosophically misstated can be philosophically corrected. Logicians rightly have endeavored to point out the many *non sequiturs* that lead to the conclusion — "Hence an omnipotent, omniscient, good God cannot exist." A remedial strategy alone does not suffice, however, particularly not when its authors fail to question the more fundamental anthropomorphic premises that inspired the objections. But even those who succeed in replacing a simplistic conception of God by a philosophically more coherent one do not dispel our basic doubt whether *any* kind of *autonomous* philosophical speculation would be capable of meeting a difficulty born in metaphysical despair. The philosopher may, of course, dismiss such doubts as unreasonable and insist that on his terrain the discussion must be restricted by the clearly defined limits of logical argument.

To be sure, such basic work is needed. But a more fundamental problem remains: theodicy is based upon a concept of religion in which the believer will hardly recognize his or her own. As Kant defined it, theodicy consists in "the defense of the supreme wisdom of the Creator [*Urheber*] of the world against the charges raised by reason on the basis of what conflicts with a meaningful order [*Zweckwidrig*] in the world."[2] The God hereby presented is not merely "less" than the "Father" whom Jesus revealed or than the God of Israel: he essentially differs from either. To be sure, there is nothing wrong with an attempt to articulate philosophically the dependence of creation on God, while leaving all other aspects out of consideration. If finite being

---

1. Arthur Schopenhauer, *The World as Will and Representation,* supplemental chap. 17 (added to Section 15).

2. Kant, *Werke* (Berlin Akademie ed.), 8:255.

depends on an omnipotent, wise Creator, that dependence is worth investigating. The problem begins, however, when that dependence is conceived exclusively in terms of *efficient* causality. The link between God and the creature is obviously more intimate than that between an efficient cause (as modern thought conceived of it) and its effect.[3] To represent it exclusively in causal terms makes it extremely difficult, if not impossible, to justify any suffering avoidable in the creation of an all-wise, omnipotent God. The so-called physico-theological argument, whereby the mind proves the existence of God on the basis of the cosmos, becomes then inverted into a normative rule that determines the limits of divine action in the world. One of the modes in which God relates to creation comes thereby to function as the very standard of his activity with respect to the cosmos and all that is in it.

A theodicy based upon such a narrowly conceived, purely causal relation differs, of course, from the older one that rested upon a more inclusive relationship between God and creation. In the following pages I intend to return to that older tradition (medieval and in part already Platonic) by taking account of other, specifically religious modes of conceiving that relation. Such an approach, though more modest in its claims than the rationalist one tends to be, may in the end prove more religiously appropriate and therefore also more fruitful. As Brian Hebblethwaite observed: "One has actually to meet religious people, Buddhists, Hindus, Christians, Jews, Muslims, and see how they in fact confront the world's evil, if one is going to grasp something of the resources of religion for coping with suffering and wrong."[4] It should be clear from the outset that to adopt this approach is not to renege on philosophical theology, but to expand it beyond the rationalist limits within which a purely causal, basically deist philosophy has constrained it. The method of philosophy imposes certain restrictions upon such a use of "dogmatic" material, for unless the philosopher detaches his religious sources from the absolute authority they enjoy within the religious community, philosophy loses its autonomy and becomes transformed into theology. Scripture, theology, and mystical speculation provide *models* for conveying a concrete

3. I have developed this point in "Transcendance et objectivisme" in *Archivio di Filosofia* (Rome, 1977), pp. 265-72.

4. Brian Hebblethwaite, *Evil, Suffering and Religion* (London: Sheldon Press, 1976), p. 10.

content to our relation with a transcendent absolute.[5] They do not replace critical reflection.

A further challenge confronting a religiously "inclusive" approach is that the religious sources that direct its search date from a remote past and often present an anthropomorphic image of God that today's educated believer may find hard to take as literal truth. This applies, of course, most obviously to the older books of the Bible, but even the more recent ones of the New Testament create problems of interpretation. A literal reading of some of the historical narratives may add considerably to the difficulties of a philosophical theodicy, rather than reduce them. I must confess that in this respect I find the methods of those Christian philosophers who commendably react against a deist rationalism often seriously wanting in the interpretation of ancient texts. Too many appear unwilling to accept that the meaning of a text lies in the total context. Applied to canonical texts dating from a remote past this principle would appear to require some acquaintance not only with the literal context, but also with the historical one. The meaning of a passage in archaic writings such as the books of the Pentateuch cannot be gathered by the same methods that we use for analyzing a modern study of history. To treat an ancient narrative as a critically historical discourse can only set philosophical reflection on the wrong track from the start. One may attempt to extricate oneself from those self-inflicted problems by arguing that none of the improbable assumptions inherent in a literal reading is "demonstrably false."[6] But no discipline known to me has ever profited from accepting highly unlikely claims as true as long as they cannot be positively demonstrated to be false.

On the opposite side, however, the question arises whether a rationally "edited" reading of ancient sacred texts would not lead us right back to the kind of rationalist theodicy we are trying to avoid. Can we escape being rationalists when we leave out what cultural or

5. For a justification of such a "hypothetical" use of intrinsically religious sources in philosophy the reader may consult my "Blondel's Reflection on Experience," in *A Dubious Heritage: Philosophy of Religion after Kant* (New York: Paulist Press, 1977).

6. As Eleanore Stump does in "The Problem of Evil," *Faith and Philosophy* 2 (1985): 392-423, where she makes the highly dubious claim concerning the Cain and Abel story in Genesis: "To the extent to which Christians are committed to accepting the Bible as the revealed word of God, to that extent they are committed to accepting this story as veridical also" (p. 413). "Veridical" here stands for historically true.

personal taste finds hard to accept? Which principles enable us to discern the essential, religious message from the anthropomorphic metaphor? What must be the criterion for responsibly reading the Bible as an account of divine action? To eliminate all anthropomorphism, as the Enlightenment attempted, leaves us with no more than the lifeless skeleton on which deism built its idea of God. Moreover, it would implicitly deny the most fundamental datum of Jewish, Christian, and Moslem religious anthropology, namely, that God has created human beings in his own image and likeness. Despite these difficulties I do not believe that preserving the authority of the Bible forces us literally to accept the more primitive metaphors in which the message has been concretely presented. Among them we count biblical images of God's all too human emotions (jealousy, anger, etc.), his abrupt, by human standards arbitrary decisions and subsequent repentance, his creation of cosmos and persons in the manner of physical fashioning (in Genesis 2, as a potter working with clay). It is not possible to define once and for all at which point representations become unacceptably anthropomorphic. The rational demands of interpretation develop under the impact of new scientific theories about cosmos and person, but also of theological and metaphysical refinement. What to the J writer of Genesis appeared perfectly acceptable may no longer appear so to us. Yet it seems not unreasonable to assume the general principle that a representation becomes unsatisfactory when even serious believers perceive it as conflicting with the ideas of God, person, and cosmos that centuries of philosophical, theological, and scientific reflection have left us. It would be difficult conclusively to demonstrate the falsehood of such representations, as fundamentalist interpreters challenge us to do. Yet much of what is not demonstrably false may strike an educated believer in our time as improbable beyond falsehood. At least in the area of theodicy little may be gained from the use of canonical texts in support of representations that believing philosophers would find it hard to accept as literal truth. Even if such representations are no more than highly improbable to the educated, they cease to be useful for the particular task of theodicy that consists in making the idea of God more (rather than less) acceptable in the face of evil.

Finally, and most importantly, we must remind ourselves that not all religious traditions share the same assumptions about the origin and significance of evil, and hence that there is no single

"religious answer" to evil. Positions vary from a strong affirmation
of evil as an ultimate principle coequal with the good in Manicheism,
to a denial of its reality as an illusion in the more radical Buddhist
and Vedantic monist schools. Between these two extremes theist
responses range from an evil inherent in the finite condition as such,
to evil as the sole responsibility of the human race (through the fall
and subsequent sins). Of course, evil provokes the strongest reaction
among such monotheists as Jews, Christians, and Moslems, who
consider all finite being the creation of a free God. The confrontation
with evil in God's creation has spawned a variety of responses.
Judaism alone presents several models. According to the archaic
retaliation model, God inflicts suffering as a punishment for human
sin. But, one might wonder, why should humans, created by God,
commit sin? Israel never ceased to struggle with this question, and
many felt compelled to look in a different direction. One alternative
model delays the overcoming of evil until a future time of history.
But why should creation have to pass through evil in order to reach
a happy ending? In the face of such major difficulties two different
models emerged. The Book of Job concludes that humans are not
in a position to question God's inscrutable decrees, while Deutero-
Isaiah, in his description of the suffering servant, abstains from
seeking the sinful origin of suffering and considers suffering itself
intrinsically redemptive.

Christianity adopted all four of these models but connected the
idea of punishment primarily to Adam's fall, while grounding the idea
of redemptive suffering in the passion and death of Christ. In addition,
early theologians combined those scriptural positions with the prevailing philosophical ones (mainly Neoplatonic and Stoic). Thus they
adopted the Neoplatonic interpretation according to which evil consists in a lack of being — *privatio boni*. As John Hick has shown, this
solution, suitable for an order of being in which necessary emanations
move down from the One, causes serious difficulties in a universe
freely created by God.[7] While the Neoplatonic *One* is not responsible
for all the ills inherent in the lower hypostases that with absolute
necessity emanate from it, a free, omnipotent Creator *chooses* what is
to exist. Augustine, who was chiefly responsible for establishing this

---

7. John Hick, *Evil and the God of Love* (San Francisco: Harper & Row, 1978), pp.
70-78.

privative conception of evil in the West, attempted to counter the objection by means of a Greek aesthetics of form. Contrast, for him, including the contrast between good and evil, adds to the perfection of the created form. Needless to say, an aesthetic principle of perfection that requires the presence of physical pain and moral evil and that results in the final damnation of most moral agents hardly corresponds to the Christian idea of God's goodness or to that of the individual's responsibility. The God of love preached in the gospel of salvation here has made room for an Olympian Artist of dramatic form. Nor does one soften that grim picture much by declaring that the Creator merely *allows* moral evil, as long as one holds God to be capable of freely creating a world that contains less suffering and less moral evil. "One cannot say that God both is blameless in respect of the natural evil in our world, because He alone allows it as something inseparable from the world's good, and that He could, had He wished, have created a better world in which there would have been less natural evil."[8] Augustine obviates any divine obligation to create a better world by the idea of contrast, while he uses the *privatio boni* (hardly suitable for aesthetic contrast) to acquit God from any complicity with the evil needed for that contrast.

Created Autonomy Versus Causal Determinism

The positions that in the wake of theological and philosophical controversies came to prevail in much of Western thought under the direct or indirect impact of St. Augustine resulted in the following questionable theses.

1. God creates the intelligent agent free, yet predestines him or her to damnation or salvation.
2. The good exists as an independent value prior to the Creator's choice.
3. God remains unaffected by the finite reality.

All of these theses would at a later time and in modified form find their way into the rationalist assumptions of the theodicy formulated

8. Hick, *Evil and the God of Love,* p. 105.

in seventeenth- and eighteenth-century philosophy, which, to a great extent, is still surviving today. The modern assumptions may be summarized as follows:

1. While the Creator is the efficient cause of creation, the autonomy of the creature is severely restricted. Even the exercise of free will must somehow be determined by the causal impact of an omnipotent, omniscient Creator.
2. Ideals of goodness and value preexist our pursuit of them. The free agent may ratify or reject them, but does not constitute them.
3. The Creator stands entirely outside of his creation and remains untouched by suffering and the effects of moral evil.

The alternative model presented in this chapter rejects all three of these assumptions in favor of more authentically Christian and, I hope, more coherently philosophical principles. Yet before confronting the two models with one another we need to consider more closely the original theological theses as well as their philosophical assumptions.

The controversy over divine predestination did not reach a critical stage until the sixteenth century, when Calvin denied the exercise of free choice in the order of grace and when Thomists and Molinists initiated their acrimonious dispute *de auxiliis*. For Banez and his Thomist followers, God's position as the absolutely universal cause of creation entailed that he had to be responsible for at least a "negative reprobation" of some, previous to any personal merits and demerits. God causes no evil, but decides not to cause the good that would prevent evil from occurring. Left to its own fallen and fallible liberty, the finite will without God's efficacious grace *inevitably* sins. To this determinism Molina and his school, anxious to preserve human responsibility, opposed a free human causality next to, and partly in competition with, divine causality. These conflicting positions share the burden of an impossible task: in one case reconciling total divine causality with human responsibility for evil and, in the other, squaring total human responsibility with divine causality.

The second thesis posits the *good* as an ideal a priori, preceding God's creative act, and thus imposing upon a moral God the obligation to create the universe that approaches this ideal as closely as is possible for a finite composition. The same necessity that determines the divine being thereby extends to creation, leaving no room for either divine freedom or finite contingency. Leibniz, who formulated the position into a clearly articulated principle, attempted to escape its pantheistic implications by distinguishing between the "absolute" necessity to create the best possible world (which he denied) and the "moral" necessity by which God owed it to his goodness to create the best possible (which he affirmed). In this rationalist scenario, God contemplates the nonexistent essences of several possible worlds, after which he decides to create the actual world in accordance with his goodness — though he was not intrinsically forced to do so.[9] Even if we leave out of consideration the untenable real distinction between God's goodness and his omnipotence, we must still question Leibniz's interpretation of divine omnipotence. Does it refer to God's power to do "anything at all"? That is hardly meaningful, and Leibniz himself hastens to restrict it to what is logically possible and compossible with God's other attributes. If God is supremely good, he is not able to do evil. We should then restrict our definition of omnipotence so as to define God's ability to do anything he wills *in accordance with his divine nature*.

But even then the expression "anything he wills" raises further questions. God's "acting" expresses his nature; it does not serve, as it does for me, as a means to satisfy particular wants or desires by the attainment of goals that lie outside me. A wide gap separates what I *am* from what I attempt to attain by means of acts devised to complement my experienced deficiency. None of this applies to God. Nor am I from my own position able to conceive what God's acting implies or does not imply. All I can do is look at the concrete, visible result of that divine action that we call *creation*. But here precisely theodicy ought to follow a procedure opposite to the one it usually follows when it decrees that the world must conform to those standards of human rationality which it has a priori set up for God. A genuine, religious theodicy begins by accepting creation *as it is* (including its evil) as a visible expression of God's nature, rather than by dictating a priori what a divine expression must be like. As we shall see, such an attitude does not condemn theodicy to blind faith, for it must critically examine what it may learn of the divine nature on the basis

9. Cf. William Rowe's critical analysis, "Rationalistic Theology and Some Principles of Explanation," in *Faith and Philosophy* 1, no. 4 (1984): 361.

of this created expression, and it may conceivably conclude that this created expression fails to meet even minimal human standards of goodness. But it should do so on the basis of the total evidence (including the one provided in the specifically religious experience of faith) rather than of an a priori, narrowly rationalist definition of what God ought to be and therefore ought to do.

Returning then to Leibniz's argument, it should be clear that the idea of a divine choice with an antecedent moment of deliberation and a consequent moment of decision, patterned after the model of human persons deliberating about several alternatives, is itself heavily anthropomorphic. Kolakowski puts it well:

> In God Himself essence and existence converge and this implies that His will is identical with His essence. God neither obeys rules which are valid regardless of His will nor produces these rules according to His whims or as the result of deliberating various options; He is those rules. Unlike humans God never faces alternative possibilities and then freely decides which of them He ought to choose; His decisions are necessary aspects of His Being — and therefore they could not have been different from what they are, yet they are free in the sense that no superior powers, no norms of validity independent of God, bind Him. He *is* what He does, decides, orders. Consequently we may say neither that the definitions of what is good and true precede God, . . . nor that He precedes them.[10]

In addition to these intradivine difficulties of God "choosing" the best possible world, other difficulties are inherent in the very concept of "best possible world." Bergson pointed them out and dismissed the entire idea in a few lapidary sentences:

> I can, at a stretch, represent something in my mind when I hear of the sum-total of existing things, but in the sum-total of the non-existent I can see nothing but a string of words. So that here again the objection is based on a pseudo-idea, a verbal entity. But we can go further still: the objection arises from a whole series of arguments implying a radical defect of method. A certain representation is built up *a priori,* and it is taken for granted that this is the idea of God; from thence are deduced the characteristics that the world ought to

10. Leszek Kolakowski, *Religion* (Oxford University Press, 1982), p. 25.

show; and if the world does not actually show them, we are told that God does not exist.[11]

One imposes no undue restrictions upon divine perfection by declaring God unable to achieve what conflicts with the nature of the finite. Finite being is intrinsically imperfect and any attempt to measure its perfection depends itself on finite, hence intrinsically, imperfect norms. Thus the idea of the best possible world imposes upon the Creator a subjective, human standard.

The most serious problems begin when modern theodicy attempts to square the idea of a perfect Creator with the creation of free agents capable of perpetrating moral evil and inflicting suffering upon other creatures. On this issue the modern assumption leads to the most questionable conclusions. Both theodicy's adversaries and advocates hold a concept of freedom that from the start sets the discussion on the wrong track. Thus Antony Flew argues that for an action to be free it suffices that it not be compelled — which, for him, entails *not* that it is unpredictable, but that the person nevertheless *could* have acted differently had he chosen to do so. From these premises he concludes that an omnipotent Creator could have created persons who would always (or more often) have acted rightly.[12] J. L. Mackie concurs: human beings could have been so constituted as freely to choose the good. The idea of a God who could not control people's actions leads to what he calls the "paradox of omnipotence."[13] How the idea of a will determined always to choose the good remains compatible with freedom escapes me. Nor do I see how in a theory of predetermined freedom evil could avoid being ultimately attributable to God.[14]

Yet the most questionable concept appears to be that of a finite freedom created with a built-in resistance to evil. Freedom is far more

11. Henry Bergson, *The Two Sources of Morality and Religion,* trans. Ashley Andra and Cloudesly Brereton (Garden City: Doubleday, 1951), p. 261. See also James Felt's pertinent remarks in "God's Choice: Reflections on Evil in a Created World," *Faith and Philosophy* 1, no. 4 (1984): 370-77.

12. Antony Flew, "Divine Omnipotence and Human Freedom," in *New Essays in Philosophical Theology,* ed. Flew and MacIntyre (London: SCM Press, 1965), p. 152.

13. J. L. Mackie, "Evil and Omnipotence," *Mind* 64, no. 254 (1955): 200-212. Reprinted in *God and Evil,* ed. Nelson Pike (Englewood Cliffs, N.J.: Prentice Hall, 1964), pp. 46-60. Reference is to p. 57.

14. See Alfred North Whitehead, *Religion in the Making* (New York: Meridian Books, 1961), p. 92.

than the power to say *yes* or *no* to divinely preestablished values with or without a divine impulse toward one or the other. Its signal characteristic consists not in the power to ratify preestablished values but in the ability to create them. Freedom can tolerate contingency and an extremely restricted field of operation. But to interfere with its creative power is to replace freedom by causality. Creativity constitutes its very essence. Both theists and atheists admit freedom to be "given," but it is not given in the way of causal determination. Even a wholly preestablished order of values reduces its scope. Most of us agree on that point when it comes to humanly induced unconscious conditioning (including hypnosis), such as B. F. Skinner proposes for the improvement of society as a whole. But the same objection holds true for any divine "conditioning." Even a divinely preestablished order leaves a person none but a negative creativity (as Sartre perceived). Yet, strangely enough, this inauthentic, reduced freedom of choice, the very same one the secular critics of theodicy reject in predestinationist theologies, is the one they propose as the only one compatible with the existence of a good God.

God creates neither values nor strong or weak inclinations to choose them; he creates creators who depend on a divine source for the exercise of their creative spontaneity, but not for its determination. Nor need such a theory result in the kind of atheism it has entailed in some existentialist philosophies. For an essential part of the free agent's creative project consists in practically recognizing his overall *dependence*. Failure to do so deprives us of an absolute in determining the hierarchy of values, while forcing us to elevate relative values into absolutes. Now, a freedom responsible for creating its own values remains intrinsically and irrevocably able to erect false absolutes and even to invert the creative impulse into an annihilating power. Genuine freedom is endowed with a capacity unlimited for evil as well as for good. In creating free agents God has released a power that may turn against himself. In Berdyaev's words: "Evil presupposes freedom and there is no freedom without the freedom of evil, that is to say, there is no freedom in the state of compulsory good."[15] Leibniz understood this better than some of his followers.

15. Nicholas Berdyaev, *The Divine and the Human,* trans. R. M. French (London: Geoffrey Bles, 1948), p. 92.

The real issue concerning freedom is not whether it deserved to be created, but whether God's necessary being is compossible with such an unrestricted creaturely autonomy as freedom requires. Since that issue obviously falls outside the limits of theodicy, we need not enter into it. Nor should theodicy solve the question of the existence of spiritual beings endowed with a clearer sense of freedom's potential and therefore less inclined to pervert its creative autonomy (e.g., angels). Its own question concerns the compatibility of free agents *as we know them* with the existence of a good and wise Creator. Moreover, theodicy should be concerned only with the *compatibility* of the world *as it is,* not with the possibility of proving the existence of God on the basis of this world's perfection. Symptomatic for the confusion that often occurs between the two is that many modern treatises of theodicy begin with a discussion of Hume's *Dialogues Concerning Natural Religion.* Whatever Hume's intention may have been, he did not write an antitheodicy, that is, a refutation of any possibility to defend the idea of God in the face of evil in creation. The *Dialogues* deflate the exaggerated claims of a natural theology that by means of a purely philosophical speculation concerning order and purpose in the world concludes to the existence of God. Even on those terms we should beware of overstating the case. Does Philo, the most skeptical of the three participants in the dialogue, after having invalidated all arguments presented in favor of a benevolent Providence, not concede in the end: "In many views of the universe and of its parts, particularly the latter, the beauty and fitness of final causes strike us with such irresistible force, that all objections appear (what I believe they really are) mere cavils and sophisms; nor can we then imagine how it was ever possible for us to repose any weight on them."[16] One may, of course, dismiss this statement as the expression of a thorough skepticism whereby Philo, after having first invalidated the arguments of the other interlocutants, in the end scuttles his own. But we may also read this as a sincere attempt to attain "synoptically," that is, by an immediate, total impression, what analytic inference withholds. If this reading is correct, an "illative sense" would provide what analysis alone fails to supply, namely certitude concerning the existence of an intelligent Designer who

16. Hume, *Dialogues Concerning Natural Religion,* ed. N. Kemp Smith (Indianapolis: Library of the Liberal Arts, 1947), p. 202.

may be infinitely perfect and good (though these attributes cannot be established by natural reason alone).[17]

The implications of Hume's argument so understood would be less constrictive for philosophical theodicy than that of much contemporary fideism, which, rightly dissatisfied with the rationalist theodicy, prefers to leave the justification of God in the face of evil entirely to faith. The philosopher cannot remain satisfied with such a total abdication of reason: the presence of evil must be *shown* not to exclude the idea of a good Creator. Nor will the philosopher be satisfied with defining "divine goodness" by standards that have nothing in common with our human conception of goodness, an equivocity that, as John Stuart Mill pointed out, would merely result in "an incomprehensible attribute of an incomprehensible substance."[18] The philosopher rightly insists that the idea of an omnipotent, good God be shown to be compatible with the actual existence of evil. Reason modestly yet legitimately demands only to perceive how an open conflict between a good God and an evil world is *not inevitable*.

Philosophy cannot meet even that modest goal unless it adequately answers the objection of God's supreme indifference to the suffering of his creatures. To do so becomes nearly impossible for one who accepts the third of the Augustinian theses, especially after it became combined with the idea of the Creator as efficient cause in the modern sense. Even medieval scholasticism in denying any real relation between God and the world had placed itself in an unfavorable position for defending the Creator against the charge of supreme indifference. For such a defense to be effective philosophy would have to accept that the sufferings of creation, including the suffering caused by human evil, affect the Creator himself. A number of philosophical systems broadly comprehended under the general name of "process philosophy" have attempted to justify such a divine participation in finite processes. Despite essential disagreements concerning the relation between the finite and the infinite, divine personhood, and the role and ultimate destiny of human individuals, all these systems share Whitehead's overall vision of the real as a creative process, whereby

17. I owe the comparison with Newman's "illative sense" (who was undoubtedly influenced by Hume) to Steven Fields.

18. John Stuart Mill, *An Examination of Sir William Hamilton's Philosophy* (London: Longmans, Green, 1872), p. 128.

God comes to be *with* his creation rather than *above* it. In Whitehead's terms: "He shares with every new creation its actual world."[19] Indeed, only through the creative process does God attain that full actuality to which Whitehead refers as God's "consequent" nature. Rather than being an unchanging, transcendent Prime Mover, God is the actual entity from which each creative development in time "receives that initial aim from which its self-causation starts."[20] Various philosophers have interpreted this divine participation in various ways, ranging from an impersonal "creative event," the source of all human good (Wieman), to a creative personalism (Brightman). But only when the idea of a personal God is preserved can process philosophy contribute toward making more acceptable the monotheist position with respect to evil.

Peter Bertocci in *The Goodness of God* shows a clear appreciation of the importance of safeguarding this personal character. He bases his argument on the premise that a creative force resulting in human persons must itself be personal. But such a Creator-Person need not be conceived as self-sufficient, uninhibited by restraints other than those he imposes upon himself. If personhood reaches its highest realization in interpersonal communication, then the perfection of the divine Creator would likewise be enhanced, rather than weakened, in responding to persons. Furthermore, such a divine Person exposes himself to risks analogous to those run by humans in their attempts to create good — what Bertocci calls "creative insecurity." "Insecurity inheres in the very nature of being a person whose actual freedom of personal choice is involved in the pursuit of truth and goodness. Intrinsic to the good for persons is the insecurity that can become creative, because values are compenetrating, and because persons themselves can choose orchestration-within-pattern as they change and grow."[21] Bertocci supports this bold application of the personalist principle to the Absolute by an even more daring thesis. As he reads

19. Alfred North Whitehead, *Process and Reality* (New York: Macmillan, 1929), p. 521.

20. Whitehead, *Process and Reality,* p. 374.

21. Peter Bertocci, *The Goodness of God* (Washington, D.C.: University Press of America, 1981), p. 267. John Dewey made the point in a general way when writing: "No mode of action can . . . give anything approaching absolute servitude; it provides insurance but no assurance." *The Quest for Certainty* (1929; New York: G. P. Putnam's Sons, Capricorn Books, 1960), p. 33.

it, the insecurity of the creative act expresses a fundamental uncertainty in the very nature of the Creator-Person. A refractory element, not a "flaw" in the divine or an impediment *imposed* upon the divine, but the essential *passivity* inherent in the very act whereby the Absolute gives birth to the relative, prevents the Creator from achieving his goals without at the same time having to allow the possible intrusion of suffering and evil.

A Passive, Suffering God

In this section I intend to show that such an idea of a God who renders himself passive in the act of creation presents a more solid, as well as a more concretely religious basis for theodicy than a first cause untouched by the suffering of creation and unmoved by the effects of moral evil. The doctrine of the passion and death of Christ lends indirect, though strong, support to this position, as it rests upon the very notion of God who suffers and dies. But in all three monotheist faiths mystical and theosophical traditions have held that with creation some passivity enters God's very essence. For infinite, perfect Being to give rise to being other than itself means not adding to itself (as St. Thomas already clearly stated: *non datur plus esse*), but causing an emptiness within its own fullness wherein "otherness" can subsist. Only through an "annihilation" (Blondel) of infinite Being can the finite be *another* being. Though finite being must remain *within* the infinite, perfect Being from which it draws its entire sustenance, as *other* it assumes a certain independence. By allowing it to be in its own right, infinite Being ceases to wield unlimited power over it and comes to stand in a relation that is no longer exclusively active.

Philosophers who adopt Aristotle's definition of God as pure act tend to exclude passivity from God as incommensurable with divine perfection. Yet if we understand *pure act* as the opposite of passivity, it becomes itself imperfect. For to "act," as opposed to being acted upon, means to "re-act" to events and circumstances in a manner that forces the acting subject to go out toward the other rather than itself in order to return to itself in a different manner. Obviously, this kind of acting, wherein the agent thus loses himself in order to find himself anew, does not apply to God *as he is in himself.* Resting within itself, a perfect, infinite Being as such cannot be called active any more than passive, as Nicholas of Cusa showed in his theory of the divine coincidence of opposites. In creation, however, the two moments of activity and passivity simultaneously emerge. Though the act of creation itself requires no external support and in this respect may be called entirely "active," in the very "otherness" of the created being, God places himself in a position where he is forced to react and thereby to relate passively as well as actively. Aristotelians avoid this conclusion by asserting that God has no *real* relation to the world. But such a claim, intelligible enough within Aristotle's theory of an uncreated cosmos, makes little sense within a creationist theology.

On the other side, to introduce passivity in God and autonomy in the creature is not sufficient for solving the problem of theodicy. Indeed, even the deist with his remote, laissez-faire God implicitly or explicitly holds that, once having created the world, God leaves all initiative to the creatures, restricting his own activity to preservation and support. If there were no further divine intervention, the issue would, once again, be reduced to the simple dilemma we have rejected in the first part: Either the world is as good as it can possibly be (and to be so, however imperfect, is better than not to be, in which case God is justified), or the world could have been better than it is (and we must then conclude that an omnipotent, wise, and good God did not create it). For the believer, the "passivity" of the Creator is of a very different nature. Rather than creating and then leaving creation to its own devices, God never stops *reacting* to the creature's initiative. Monotheist theologies have expressed the interaction between God and creation in several ways. Christians affirm this ever-renewed divine action by saying that God *redeems* what he has created. Unfortunately, in theodicy believers often use the concept of redemption for stopping the gaps of ignorance that remain after they have depleted their supply of rational justifications for suffering and evil. Thus they end up yielding to the duplicity which Mill denounced, by calling "good" in an invisible order (that in a future world may become manifest) what by ordinary standards cannot but count as "bad." Rather than whitewash evil by such an *argumentum ex ignorantia* — as irrefutable as it is unprovable — the believer should, from the start, admit that this world contains a great deal of unexplainable suffering, that creatures endowed with a free will remain perfectly capable of causing unqualified evil and often avail themselves of this possibility.

Rather than use the term "redemption" to make suffering and evil vanish into an invisible realm of goodness, the Christian philosopher ought to show what the ordinary faithful have always maintained, namely that in his redemptive action God *reacts* to real suffering and real evil. To be effective in theodicy the idea of redemption must be integrated with that of creation as one continuous, active relation of God to his creatures. Such a view, contrary to the deist's, envisions divine activity as an open-ended, ever-renewed dialogue with creation. At each moment of time God creatively responds to the conditions shaped by his creatures in the preceding moment. A divine response then counteracts existing evil by constantly presenting us with new occasions for the accomplishment of good or the redemption of evil — without having to interfere with the creature's autonomy. God's response provides ever novel opportunities for converting evil into goodness. Christian writers have consistently upheld this divine ability to restore creation to new innocence. Thus Jacques Maritain suggestively argues: "Each time that a free creature undoes for its part the work that God makes, God remakes to that extent — for the better — this work and leads it to higher ends. Because of the presence of evil on earth, everything on earth, from the beginning to the end of time, is in perpetual recasting."[22] To be sure, the ways in which God actively counteracts evil in a creation increasingly threatened by it cannot be "justified" on the basis of an abstract concept of human nature. Theology may inform us that God offers ever new opportunities for converting past evil into future goodness. It may show how, in a condition antagonistic to good, such a reversal must necessarily take the form of a struggle, an *agon.* According to Christian doctrine, God himself had to provide both the means and the model of this conversion by suffering and dying under the power of evil. But in thus linking the mystery of evil to the even greater mystery of redemption we have decidedly left the domain of philosophy and introduced considerations not available to a purely philosophical reflection on reality as it is universally manifest.

The admission of dogmatic doctrines into a universal, philosophical reflection ought to be justified more thoroughly than this chapter

22. Jacques Maritain, *God and the Permission of Evil,* trans. Joseph Evans (Milwaukee: Bruce, 1966), p. 86.

allows.[23] Here I mention only one critically significant reason that forces us to admit them at least to some extent. The very standards by which we measure what does and what does not count as "good" depend upon the acceptance or rejection of an intrinsically religious hierarchization of values. Any attempt to erect a system of values upon a religiously neutral basis, common to believers and unbelievers, fails precisely in the area where theodicy matters most, namely in deciding what must count as *definitive* evil. Marilyn McCord Adams has shown how ontological commitments affect descriptions of values. Moral theories that omit any reference to a transcendent norm differ from value systems ruled by a relation to transcendent Being. More specifically, varying ontological commitments "widen or narrow the range of options for defeating evil with good."[24] The believer, not satisfied with exclusively immanent goods, may value an intimate sense of God's presence, acquired through much pain and suffering, more highly than a satisfaction of immediate needs. But different value systems result in different judgments concerning standards of good and evil.[25] In his evaluation of what constitutes unnecessary evil and what constitutes ultimate goodness, the believer often fundamentally disagrees with the nonbeliever. Diametrically opposed attitudes concerning the desirability of terminating an unwanted pregnancy become intelligible only if we take this fundamental disagreement on values into account. To recognize major differences in the perception of what in the final analysis constitutes evil need not result in the kind of verbal equivocity on good and evil denounced by J. S. Mill. Yet it should caution us against deciding prematurely what must count as *unredeemably* evil and what as *unconditionally* good. Once we introduce value judgments based on factors that fall beyond the range of a "common" appraisal of what benefits or harms human nature, we admit intrinsically private factors that make a *universal* philosophical theodicy, identical for believers and unbelievers, impossible.

Instead of continuing to attempt such an impossible enterprise,

23. For a more substantial discussion, see Louis Dupré, *The Other Dimension* (New York: Doubleday, 1972), chap. 3, "Religious Faith and Philosophical Reflection."

24. Marilyn McCord Adams, "Problems of Evil: More Advice to Christian Philosophers," in *Faith and Philosophy* 5 (April 1988): 129.

25. Alvin Plantinga argued for this position already in "The Probabilistic Argument from Evil," *Philosophical Studies* 35 (1979): 46-47.

the believing philosopher should not hesitate to include the redemptive vision of his faith in his speculation. From that broadened perspective the experience of evil and suffering, however burdensome,
can never lead to a final conclusion concerning life's balance of good
and evil. Nor is such a position based upon a purely fideist anticipation
of future well-being. For the believer may actually experience suffering itself as redemptive, that is, as endowed with more than a merely
negative meaning. "Grace and nature not being two closed worlds,
but two worlds open to one another and in mutual communication,
it might happen that the greater progress (of the wheat over that of
the cockle) would occur more in the order of grace than in that of
nature."[26] To refer to different modes of experiencing is not to ad-
vance an unsupported claim, but merely to assert what eminent psy-
chologists, beginning with William James, have persistently asserted.

The distinction here proposed finds unambiguous theological
support in the doctrine of redemptive suffering that for Jews, Christians, and Moslems transforms the meaninglessness of suffering and
evil into different patterns of meaning and goodness. In its most
radical form, expressed in the New Testament theology of Christ's
passion and death, the mystery of redemptive suffering allows God
himself to participate in human distress. No writer has pursued the
theme of suffering redemptive through God's participation in it
further than Dostoevski. Essays on theodicy routinely refer to Ivan
Karamazov's charge against a God who tolerates unredeemable suffering — the pain of innocent children and animals who lack the capacity
to learn from pain. Usually they fail to mention Alyosha's later reply.
Alyosha admits the full scandal of innocent pain and, even as his
brother, refuses to accept it. But he assumes this scandal into the even
greater one of God's own suffering. When, dying on the cross, Christ
feels abandoned by his Father, the tragic conflict enters God's own
Being. In this intradivine *theologia crucis* God is set against God, as in
Goethe's dark saying: *Nemo contra Deum nisi Deus ipse* ("No one against
God but God himself").[27] In Christ God assumes all human suffering
and takes upon himself the burden of compensating for all moral evil.
In addition, as the legend of the Grand Inquisitor suggests, God faces

26. Maritain, *God and Permission of Evil,* p. 89.
27. Cf. Luigi Pareyson, "La sofferenza inutile in Dostoevskij," *Giornale di meta-
fisica* 4 (1982): 123-70.

the failure of a salvation that surpasses the capacity for acceptance of most of those to whom it is offered. This greater scandal does not "justify" evil, but it makes God a participant in our pain, as Christian theologies have consistently implied, and mystical and theosophical ones have explicitly stated.

Gnostic and theosophical doctrines in the three monotheist religions have, in an even more daring way than Christian orthodoxy, introduced the mystery of evil into God's inner life. In contrast to orthodox beliefs, they attribute the possibility of evil (though not its actuality) to an intradivine multiplicity the harmony of which became disturbed by an unknown cause. The resulting conflict gave birth to that realm of unrest and disharmony which is the physical universe.[28] Variously formulated in Jewish, Christian, and pagan myths during the first centuries of our era, this gnostic doctrine found its most radical expression in kaballah mysticism, as it developed between the thirteenth century (the Zohar) and the sixteenth century (Isaac Luria). The German theosophist Jacob Boehme attempted to incorporate it in Lutheran theology by presenting the intradivine conflict as an opposition between God's wrath and God's mercy.[29] We hear a final major echo of it in Blake's *Prophetic Books,* according to which a fragmentation of the divine harmony has caused an intradivine conflict resulting in the creation of the physical universe.[30]

We may of course dismiss such daring speculations as unworthy of philosophical attention. But before doing so we ought to consider that major philosophers, beginning with Plato, have persistently turned to ancient mythical and religious interpretations that trace the origin of good and evil to a single transcendent source. Even some

28. Cf. Hans Jonas, *The Gnostic Religion* (Boston: Beacon Press, 1963). See also Claude Tresmontant: *A Study of Hebrew Thought* (New York: Desclee de Brouwer, 1960), esp. pp. 13-14, for a comparison with more orthodox Christian and Jewish theologies of creation.

29. Jacob Boehme, *Six Theosophic Points,* trans. John Earle (Ann Arbor: University of Michigan, 1958). See also Heinrich Bornkamm, *Luther and Boehme* (Bonn, 1925), and Cyril O'Regan: *The Trinity in Hegel's Philosophy* (Ph.D. diss., Yale University, 1989), chap. 7.

30. "Without contraries is no progression. Attraction and repulsion, reason and energy, love and hate are necessary to human existence. From the contraries spring what the religious call good and evil. Good is the passive that obeys reason; evil is the active springing from energy." William Blake, *The Marriage of Heaven and Hell* (beginning).

modern philosophers have attempted to trace the opposition between good and evil to a separation of complementaries harmoniously united in the Absolute. Thus in Karl Jaspers's memorable treatment of "The Law of the Day and the Passion for the Night," night and day appear as two complementary elements within the Absolute: intelligible but limited clarity and dark desire of the infinite. The diurnal law "regulates our existence, demands clarity, consistency, and loyalty, binds us to reason and to the idea, to the One and to ourselves."[31] The night functions as the negative desire to transcend finitude, limit, temporality. Though irreducible to the law of the day, the passion for the night is an equally essential constituent of human existence. In mythical (and highly controversial) language such reflections on complementarity within the Absolute articulate what I have described as the "passivity" that enters infinite Being when it gives birth to the finite. Orthodox monotheist theologies have never accepted the gnostic equation of creation with the fall. Nor do they accept conflicts "within" the Godhead to account for the existence of evil in creation. Rightly so, because the gnostic myths and their theosophical interpretations result in theological inconsistencies as well as in morally problematic positions. But the underlying assumption that the *possibility* of evil cannot be explained unless we trace it back to the divine act of creation itself rests on a profound insight, no more irrational than God's own participation in human suffering.

Still, the philosopher cannot but wonder what such theosophical speculations contribute to the kind of strictly rational reflection he or she is committed to. Passivity in God and otherness in the creature neither explain the actual origin of physical evil nor justify its existence. Neither do gnostic or theosophical doctrines provide the philosopher with such an explanation or justification. It would be unreasonable to expect from them rational explanations that reason itself has been powerless to provide. Theosophical doctrines do not reduce the "mysteriousness" of evil. If anything, they deepen it. What they may accomplish, however, is to extend the boundaries within which theology and the philosophy that has followed its lead conceive of that mystery. While the traditional theistic position has attributed the source of evil entirely to the creature — either as a result of sin

31. Karl Jaspers, Philosophy, vol. 3, trans. E. B. Ashton (Chicago: University of Chicago Press, 1971), p. 90.

or as an inevitable effect of finitude, theosophical doctrines force us to consider also the divine act of creation itself and the momentous transition it constitutes in Being from the one to the many. This very transition entails the possibility of opposition (and suffering!) not only *among* differently disposed and variously oriented creatures but even *within* each single living organism with its own multiplicity of tendencies, drives, and instincts.

Theosophical doctrines, however, tend to go beyond tracing the mere *possibility* of physical evil to the creative act. Most of them attribute the *actuality* of evil to a mysterious darkness within God's nature. Here philosophy cannot and should not follow them. Claims of a revelation, altogether inaccessible to reason, have no legitimate place in philosophy. Any appeal to a "secret" knowledge restricted to a special enlightenment reserved to a few remains in principle incompatible with the public goals and universal methods of philosophical reflection. Nor could such privileged enlightenment constitute an additional source of positive knowledge for the theistic philosopher. Gnostic speculation can do no more than open up perspectives different from the ones traditionally considered and invite the philosopher to explore them within his or her own discipline. In the case of physical evil it draws attention to the divine creative act itself. Such a reorientation of the philosophical attention may be highly useful for the conception of new, more fruitful models in defining the issue. Specifically, in theodicy it may force us to think of the creative act as being more complex than a simple divine *fiat.* Since the purview of this chapter limits it to a critique of traditional approaches and a suggestion of an alternative model for theodicy, this is not the proper place to develop its philosophical consequences. But it appears that a philosophical theology of the process type would be better equipped to accommodate the inherent ambiguity of the creative act with respect to physical evil than one of the traditional type, which too absolutely separates the Creator from his creation.

Conclusion

Any rational reflection on a mystery that attains its full poignancy only within religion itself requires that we take the concrete religious context of faith into consideration. As Hegel once remarked, only in actual worship are believers capable of overcoming evil. The theologically inclusive model of theodicy here defended differs from those philosophical theodicies which allege to be based upon a rational, but in fact rationalist, idea of God, far removed from living faith, if not in actual conflict with it. Theological inclusiveness does not force us to abandon the rational methods and goals of philosophy. True enough, on the cross philosophy suffers shipwreck, believers and unbelievers unanimously declare. But that does not dispense the believing philosopher from the task of showing that, within a concrete, *theological* context, belief in a good God is compatible with the existence of evil. In addition, the philosopher must examine whether the theological theses that form the context for the believer's concrete evaluation of what must count as a good or an evil remain in conformity with reason. Interpretations of Jesus' redemptive suffering as a satisfaction exacted by an angry God or a ransom paid to the devil do not satisfy that demand. But no such objections can be raised against the central Christian idea of God uniting himself to finite nature and descending in person into the abyss of human suffering and moral evil. In taking account of the mystery of evil and redemption, as faith presents it and as the believer, to a greater or lesser extent, actually *experiences* it, the Christian philosopher admits a complexity of the issue which the rationalist ignores. In giving birth to the finite, God himself inevitably assumes a certain passivity in regard to the autonomy of finite being, a passivity that may render him vulnerable and that indeed, according to the Christian mystery of the Incarnation, has induced him personally to share the very suffering of finite being.

PART II

Religious Symbolization

Religious Symbolism and Aesthetic Form

Divine Form

In New York, at the northern end of the city, on a plateau overlooking the Hudson Valley, stands my favorite museum, The Cloisters. In the heart of it a mysterious room contains the famous Unicorn Tapestries of the late Middle Ages. To visit that room is at once an enriching and an extremely disconcerting experience. As in a dense literary text literal meanings are indissolubly mingled with symbolic ones. Reality itself here is presented as a Scripture, inviting a never-ending commentary. Divinely endowed with inexhaustible spiritual significance, it constantly shifts from one meaning to another. All things refer to one another in a play of continually transformed analogies and affinities. Foucault's description of sixteenth-century attitudes applies also, and probably more so, to the late medieval vision: "Knowledge consisted in relating one form of language to another form of language; in restoring the great, unbroken plain of words and things; in making everything speak. That is, in bringing into being, at a level above that of all marks, the secondary discourse of commentary."[1] Meanings are *given,* not invented, but none are given simply. Hence, unlike what happens in a symbolization constituted by the mind, we are unable to predict the many ways in which reality may symbolize. Nature itself appears as symbolic in its very essence, rather than *rendered* symbolic

---

1. Michel Foucault, *The Order of Things* (1966; New York: Vintage Books, 1973), p. 40.

67

by the mind. We are wont to attribute all meaning to human reflection. That meaning may remain opaque — even impenetrable. Yet rarely do we question its human origin, least of all when we confront "symbolic" meaning.

Not that the medieval conception of reality excludes literalness. Long ago the eminent French historian of art, Emile Mâle, cautioned against a *purely* symbolic interpretation of the images in the French cathedral. The medieval sculptor delights in poking fun at what he deeply venerates, and at any opportunity attempts to place a not too conspicuous signature. But the "symbolism" is so intertwined with reality that the very term, as we use it, hardly applies to a world that in its entirety is perceived as *mirroring* God's complex reality. Alain de Lille's well-known verses express the matter perfectly:

Omnis mundi creatura
Quasi liber et pictura
Nobis est et speculum.

Nature indeed functioned "like a book" *(quasi liber)* in which even the illiterate could read God's writing. Medieval learning depended heavily on exegesis and knowledge and consisted mainly in "commentary" on the two books of nature and Scripture. As Foucault remarked, such a universal "commentary" assumes that every word and every thing possesses more than one meaning, that both are endowed with inexhaustible meaning that allows them endlessly to refer to one another by means of analogy and affinity.[2] Like Scripture, which conceals as much as it reveals, reality presents us with the task of decoding a revelatory text — "the book in which the Creative Trinity shines, is thought and read"[3] — by means of linguistic interpretation. To understand the book of nature fully we need the key of Scripture. Yet nature communicates meaning in its own manner. Scripture conveys meaning to nature; nature content to Scripture.

In medieval culture, no less than in modern, without language nature would have been doomed to remain symbolically silent. But the language itself appears as an integral part of creation, not as a separate universe of discourse that enables the human interpreter to reshape the meaning of nature at random. Language and nature con-

2. Foucault, *Order,* pp. 28-29.
3. St. Bonaventure, *In Hexaemeron* 12:14.

stitute two complementary parts of one divine creation, of which one articulates the manifold meanings inherent in the other.

Precisely this link between nature and language, that is, between reality and human symbolization, was dissolved at the end of the Middle Ages. We usually hold nominalist philosophy responsible for this dissolution. Once nature is reduced to the effect of an inscrutable decision of God, one can no longer expect it to coincide with the logical structure of language. Universal concepts as well as the logic built on them lose their *reality* status. The significant "proportions" among things that previously gave nature its metaphorical character exist only in thought — a thought that in the final analysis coincides with a humanly invented language. Henceforth language could become an instrument for designing *operational* concepts. To be enlisted in the service of the new observation of nature that was to give rise to modern science, words had to be stripped of all metaphoric ambiguities and reduced to atoms of universal meaning. Henceforth language more and more plays a *mediating* part between the mind and nature as given in experience. By separating speech from nature, nominalism moves in the same direction as what at first blush may appear to be its principal adversary — Italian humanism. For the humanists also, language mediated the mind with nature. Rather than turn directly to nature, they preferred to investigate first the symbolic interpretation that the classical writers had given to it. They still upheld the symbolism of the book and the need for exegesis — yet with one significant difference. While medieval symbolism had never separated language from nature (the "two books"), language now appears as a separate, ennobled, and humanized entity — a human *mirror of nature*.

As a result of the nominalist separation between language and the nature of the real as well as of the humanist creative excess of language over nature, nature lost much of the symbolic power it had possessed before. The change not only affected the nature of religious symbolization, it also undermined the "beautiful" quality the objective *forms* of religion had enjoyed in the past. This process reached completion in the eighteenth centure when what once had been considered a "transcendental," that is, a universal attribute of being as such, came to be regarded as a subjective mode of perceiving. Hence the new term "aesthetics," that is, theory of perceiving.

In his masterly seven-volume *Herrlichkeit,* translated as *The Glory of the Lord*[4] Hans Urs von Balthasar has tried to restore the ontological quality beauty had possessed during the centuries from Plato to Aquinas and, with it, to recapture the kind of objective symbolization a *religious* aesthetic requires. The Swiss thinker moves beyond the subjective perspective of modern aesthetics, without, however, denying the creative role of the human subject in language and art that distinguishes modern culture. He insists on the aesthetic *priority* of the radiating form of creation and redemption over all human creativity. That priority constitutes an essential condition for establishing the kind of *objective* symbolization that religion, especially the Christian religion, requires. His work, then, does more than restoring the ontological quality of aesthetics and integrating it with the modern view of the creative subject. It has opened the way to the understanding and renewal of religious symbols in the modern age.

Herrlichkeit starts from the traditional principle that beauty is a transcendental quality of Being itself and is, indeed, its primary manifestation. In the *form* appears the depth of Being and, to the religious mind, the presence of God. Modern aesthetics has turned away from that "sure light of Being" (St. Thomas), and has reduced poetry and art to formalist exercises or private expressions, marginal to the deeper concerns of human existence. Since religion is concerned with ultimacy, poetic and artistic form have ceased to serve as its primary expressions. Not in the subject, but in Being itself, does the aesthetic illumination of form originate. The ontological culminates in the theological. Beautiful form, beyond manifesting Being, reveals the nonmanifest depth of a divine presence (I, 443).

The essence of form lies not in its being a potential object of sense perception, but rather in its intrinsic power *to express* — whatever mode of appearance the expression may take. In the language of Christian theology that means for von Balthasar that in the Incarnation God essentially expresses himself in a *divine form*. What the form reveals in Christ and through him in all finite forms is not a direct

---

4. References to the volumes translated into English will be by Roman numeral for the volume and by Arabic number for the page. The English titles of the volumes here used are: I, *Seeing the Form* (1982); II, *Studies in Theological Style: Clerical Styles* (1984); III, *Studies in Theological Style: Lay Styles* (1986). The translation, a joint American-British enterprise, stands under the direction of Joseph Fessio, S.J., and John Riches. All volumes were originally published by Johannes Verlag in Einsiedeln (1961-1969) and, in English translation, by Ignatius Press in San Francisco.

"resemblance" between the visible and the invisible, but the fact that the divine source of this expression in visible form is itself *formally* structured. "It is in their being light and in their act of self-expression that the substances' resemblance to God lies; in this they express God, though it is rather he who expresses himself in them" (II, 346). What any given form reflects, then, is not one attribute of God or another, but God's inexhaustible, ever mysterious expressiveness itself. The form constitutes no attempt to copy its divine source, but to manifest a God who remains hidden, and precisely in its ability to do so lies its *formal* (i.e., aesthetic) perfection. Beings appear theologically "beautiful" not through a particular facet of their being but simply through their being itself. As a theological category, beauty is a *transcendental* attribute of Being itself (I, 30). No more than truth or goodness or unity, can it be lifted out of the totality of Being to mark only the privileged exception.

Still, one wonders, why should von Balthasar call any form expressive of the unmanifest Mystery "beautiful," particularly when the expression of that divine life in the Christian cross conflicts with accepted aesthetic standards? "The Christ *epiphaneia* of God has nothing about it of the simple radiance of the Platonic sun of the good. It is an act in which God utterly freely makes himself present, as he commits to the fray the last divine and human depths of love" (II, 12). Von Balthasar's theological aesthetic radically deviates from the norms of traditional theories of the beautiful. Rather than rendering his theological aesthetic a *subspecies* of that tradition which has developed from Plato to Heidegger, he has set up an *analogous* order that, while sharing the general norms of expressive form, establishes its own laws from above, so to speak. As in Eckhart's theory and in that of most Christian mystics, this analogy between the divine and the human order does not move in an ascending line (from the creatures to God), but in a descending one that views creation in a divine, revealed light. The suffering and death of Christ, far from being the exception they would be in a worldly aesthetic, here become the *model*. They have, in fact, opened new form perspectives on "the nocturnal side of existence" for which earlier theories had no place.

Yet, if the *analogia crucis* is to penetrate our entire vision of the real, it must, at some point, link up with an idea of God based upon the *analogia entis*. Revelation sets up a new analogy which, rather than abandoning transcendental aesthetics, establishes new norms and criteria for it. A theological aesthetic requires more than an inward vision: it must be able to present the world as manifesting God's presence. Hence the analogy from above must be complemented by some analogy from below. Only the latter can provide the symbols and images to make that theological vision concrete and extend it to the entire world. In modern culture this has become exceedingly difficult. More and more, faith tends to depend exclusively on revelation and/or on the inner experience. God has to be known through his revelation and through his inner voice, so to speak, in isolation from the world. Theological *form* has increasingly come to be reduced to the "formal" aspect of the expression rather than revealing itself in the very experience of the cosmic structure. Whatever divine light reaches the modern believer's mind illuminates mostly the inner realm of the soul. The separation between the realms of nature and of grace has caused a "disincarnation" of theology in the modern age.

Christian revelation constitutes a form of the Absolute that sheds new light on all other forms. It shares the aesthetic radiance inherent in all forms. Yet it differs from them in that the revealed form not merely points to the Absolute, but expresses it centrally and definitively. It transforms all other forms we perceive in its light. Comparing its effect to the inherited Greek view of the cosmos, we see it breaking down the relative identity between that cosmos and its absolute foundation. One divine *Subject* directs the manifestation of the cosmos. How the cosmos manifests the ultimate mysteriousness of Being must, in the final analysis, be learned from that divine Subject itself. Nor is the cosmos alone sufficient to manifest that mystery. In the Christian revelation the transcendental aesthetic assumes a wholly new perspective, one not given in the mind's natural perceptiveness. This transformation of our perspective on Being revolutionized Western metaphysics.

Revelation constituted "the inwardness of absolute Being, the mystery of its life and love" (I, 148), breaking forth as "the self-revelation of the mystery of Being itself" (I, 145). By the end of the Middle Ages, however, theology separated the supernatural from the natural order and thereby deprived the created form from its ability to express the divine. To restore the theological expressiveness of the natural form was the principal objective of von Balthasar's aesthetics. To be sure, the divine mystery remains intrinsically hidden: the more God reveals, the more God conceals. But revelation sheds a divine light upon nature, and in that light nature reflects God's very being. Von Balthasar finds theological support for his position in Irenaeus, who insisted, against gnostic spiritualism, on seeking the figure of grace in nature itself. The flesh is "not without the artistic wisdom and power of God," but "God's hands are accustomed, as they have been from the time of Adam, to give their work a rhythm and hold it strongly, to support and place it where they choose" (*Adv. Haereses* 2, 330-31, cited in II, 73).

Thus far the argument has simply assumed that the Christ form must provide the final principle for an aesthetic of revelation while the natural forms offer no adequate basis for such a theological aesthetic. Yet how could revelation lay a foundation for aesthetics without reducing its vision to a "natural" one? Is the very concept of the aesthetic not grounded in a natural ability to perceive "natural" forms? Von Balthasar, fully conscious of the decisive significance of this question, has devoted the most profound pages of his *opus* to an attempt to answer it. To repeat, he does not deny the relative autonomy of the natural form, but he assumes this natural aesthetic into an aesthetic of grace that, while fully respecting the autonomy of nature, nevertheless in the light of the Christian mysteries aesthetically transforms the natural. Revelation itself radiates the light in which we see its form. *In lumine tuo videbimus lumen.* "The light of faith stems from the object which revealing itself to the subject, draws it out beyond itself — into the sphere of the object" (I, 181). God's revelation establishes both its content and the believer's ability to comprehend it. Christ reveals as the God who expresses, and stands revealed as that which he expresses. Unlike the Socratic teacher he does not merely teach the truth: he *is* what he teaches. His form conceals as much as it reveals, but that concealment belongs essentially to the nature of what he reveals. The light, then, within which the believer apprehends God's manifestation entirely originates in the manifestation itself. So does the believing response to it: faith does not exist alongside of Christ's word, but is God's own response to it given by one "enacted" by God (Eph. 2:10). The believer assents "within the object of his faith" (I, 192), thereby partaking in the eternal *yes* the Son speaks to the Father. The union of the believer with Christ links the two constituent parts of the act of faith — the object and the response to it. The eye with which the believer sees God, as Eckhart forcefully expressed it, is the eye with which God sees himself. In modern

language, the conditions for the possibility of "theological" knowledge
are the very conditions that constitute the "theological" object, with
the important restriction that the object itself provides the conditions
for its knowledge. "The light of faith cannot . . . be thought or even
experienced as a merely immanent reality in our soul, but solely as
the radiance resulting from the presence in us of a *lumen increatum,* a
gratia increata, without our ever being able to abstract from God's
Incarnation" (I, 215).

As von Balthasar presents it, that faith constitutes a new way of
experiencing the world. The Eastern theology of God's uncreated
light, manifest in Jesus' transfiguration, has from the beginning proclaimed the existence of a supernatural *experience* of faith. Even in
the West, particularly in Augustine, faith originally included experience as an essential part of itself. Not until Suarez was the "supernatural" quality of that experience disputed and lowered to a psychological level. The matter is crucial to von Balthasar's thesis. If
experience does not belong to the essence of faith itself, the form
construed on the basis of that experience possesses no theological
standing whatever. A study of theological form then turns into a
branch of natural aesthetics (as it did in the aesthetic theologies of
the romantic era) wherein the form functions only as the *appearance*
of a totally different, supernatural reality. For von Balthasar, the *gnosis*
of theology grows entirely out of the experience of faith and belongs
to the same order. "Theology deepens *pistis* into *gnosis* so far as this
is possible on earth, and it does this through a contemplative pene-
tration of the depths of individual facts" (I, 601). Precisely because
it originates in the *experience* of faith theology possesses both an
aesthetic and a mystical quality. All too often modern theology has
restricted faith to a set of divinely communicated principles that
theology, then, by purely rational methods, develops into a rationally
coherent system. Following the older tradition, von Balthasar regards
faith as a comprehensive, supernatural experience in its own right
— intellectual, volitional, emotional — through which God's Spirit
takes possession of the human mind. "The 'gifts of the Holy Spirit'
bestowed seminally by grace, lead the believer to an ever deeper
awareness and experience both of the presence within him of God's
being and of the depth of the divine truth, goodness, and beauty in
the mystery of God. This experience is usually referred to as Christian *mysticism* in the most general sense of the term" (I, 166). God's

revelation, for von Balthasar as for Augustine, establishes its own *sensorium* in the soul (I, 249, 163).

Nor should this experience of faith be separated from the *natural* experience that it fulfills and transforms. The impact of the object of faith affects the mind's natural perception of Being. "Along with the ontic order that orients man and the form of revelation to one another, the grace of the Holy Spirit creates the faculty that can apprehend this form, the faculty that can relish it and find its joy in it, that can understand it and sense its interior truth and rightness" (I, 247). Faith transforms the soul's ontic dynamism into a supernatural receptivity of the revealed form. Though fulfilling the mind's natural aspirations, the experience of faith emerges from *within* faith, is conducted by the standards of faith, and results in seeing the form of faith (I, 225-27). Even as a great work of art imposes its own spiritual a priori upon the viewer or the hearer, faith, according to von Balthasar, bestows its own intrinsic necessity upon the entire natural order (I, 164).

Yet grace "imposes" its form without doing violence to nature. The revelation in Christ occurs within a divinely created nature which already in its own being manifests God's eternal presence. Hence revelation must not only adopt the form of this world; it completes that form by extending it to its ultimate archetype, God's triune nature. Hence the highest form quality of the Christ, his divine relation to the Father, stands not outside the structure of this world: it appears as a form *within* this world, yet one from which that world itself must receive its ultimate determination. Christ is not a sign pointing beyond itself to an invisible God: he himself, the indivisible God-man, is the reality he signifies, "man insofar as God radiates from him; God insofar as he appears in the man Jesus" (I, 437). Being ultimate, the Christ form becomes itself the measure of all other forms. For von Balthasar, as for Bonaventure, the Son is archetype of all creation because he is absolute expression.

The Incarnation would not constitute the definitive form if Christ's humanity had merely been a form extrinsic to God's inner life. To shed divine light upon the finite order the God-man must somehow present God's own form (I, 480). If God were wholly inexpressible, the Incarnation would have no theologically expressive significance. What Christ reveals in his own reality, however, is that intradivine relationship whereby God himself is form. "In the Son of Man then appears not God alone; necessarily there also appears the inter-trinitarian event of his procession; there appears the triune God" (I, 479). God is able to express *himself* in Jesus because he is expressive in his divine nature, and Christ's humanity, far from being a conces-sion made to human frailty in God's self-revelation, is the divine reality itself as it becomes manifest. What remains concealed in him (his divinity) has not been withdrawn from manifestation, but rather *manifests* the inscrutable, divine mystery itself. As in the work of art, no ulterior reality hides *behind* the form: the form, totally manifest, adduces its own evidential power. Incomprehensibility constitutes as much a positive property in the form of God's revelation as the continuing mystery does in a beloved person (I, 186). Both the con-cealed and the revealed become objects of the *perception* of faith. "Vis-ible form not only 'points to' an invisible, unfathomable mystery; form is the apparition of this mystery, and reveals it while, naturally, at the same time protecting and veiling it. . . . The content does not lie behind the form but within it" (I, 151). The entire mystery becomes *visible*. The religious aesthetics surpasses the dualism between the external sign of faith and the internal light: the light breaks forth from the form itself.

Ritual:
The Divine Play of Time

Gerardus Van der Leeuw once defined ritual as a game bound by rules.[1] Indeed, the analogy between rite and play appears obvious enough. Both structure our experience of time in a manner supportive of the organic rhythm of life. What in young animals serves a biological function humans have raised to the supreme expression of their dependence upon a transcendent source. Yet a clear continuity links the modest beginning with its noble end. For already the earliest form of human play defines a sacred order, while even the most solemn ceremony retains the memory of its playful origins.[2] From ancient Greece and Rome to Maya and medieval Christian cults, play and ritual celebration belonged together. Always and everywhere human beings appear to have felt a need to formalize their activity, and the measured activity of play lies at the root of that self-conscious articulation of existence that we at a later stage of development are wont to refer to as "religious" ritual. *Celebration,* the term commonly used for religious worship, still evokes the "good time" associated with play. A new order created in ritual or play endows our ordinary sense of succession with that more significant distinctness, which eventually becomes the highest norm of human activity. Into the confusion of life play intro-

1. Gerardus Van der Leeuw, *Religion in Essence and Manifestation* (1933), trans. J. E. Turner (London: Allen and Unwin, 1938; Princeton, N.J.: Princeton University Press, 1985), p. 340.
2. Johan Huizinga, *Homo Ludens,* trans. R. F. C. Hull (London: Kegan Paul, 1949), p. 17.

duces a temporary perfection, Huizinga claimed. After play and ritual have gone their own way, rites more exclusively concentrate on retrieving the important stages of existence from the passing flow of time.

Ritual in Time

Of all the burdens that a person has to carry through life, I wonder whether any weighs heavier than the transient nature of human experience. Not only does all life inevitably move toward decline and death, but the passage of time prevents any phase of human existence from ever attaining a definitive meaning. Transitoriness and oblivion mark life as a whole as well as each of its segments. In his theological anthropology, *De hominis opificio,* Gregory of Nyssa describes existence in time as an imperfect condition introduced into the plan of creation only to forestall the even more fateful consequence of instant destruction of the whole human race after the fall. In the end, however, time will be abolished and existence will once again contract to its original self-identity. The futility of life in time continues to oppress our contemporaries as much as Gregory's and the countless generations that preceded him. Nietzsche said it well: that what *was* no longer *is,* and that what is will soon no longer be, is the condition from which man most urgently desires to be saved. "To redeem those who lived in the past and to recreate all 'it was' into a 'thus I willed' — that alone should I call salvation."[3] Men and women of all ages have felt the need to order and structure the flux of time by recapturing, again and again, the founding events of the beginning. The recalling of time in archetypical gestures interpreted through sacred words would convey, so they hoped, permanent form to the indefinite continuum of their lives.

What is it that gives ritual interpreted in myth this mysterious power to regain a reversible past? What bond links the ancient narrative to the permanent gesture? We continue to ignore the answer to these fundamental questions. But whether the myth follows the rite as the reflection upon the deed, or whether the two are indissolubly

3. Nietzsche, *Thus Spoke Zarathustra,* in *The Portable Nietzsche,* ed. Walter Kaufman (New York: Viking Press, 1956), p. 281.

united in a single deed, the rite possesses a meaning of its own that resists the shifts and changes of the restless narrative. The ritual gesture must be understood in its own structured movement, not as an allegorical reenactment of an independent tale. Some religious faiths even appear to have detached ritual from myth altogether. Roman religion has traditionally been interpreted as an unimaginative imitation of Greek mythology. A more correct view is that because of its emphasis on practical efficacy and the theoretical skepticism of its followers, it has *deliberately* demythologized its rites. In any event, it is the ritual that enables the accompanying myth to reenter, across the lapse of time, into the actuality of the present. Only through the sacred gesture does the narrative of divine institution transubstantiate fugitive appearance into lasting reality. The rite alone recalls the sacred reality of the past into the present. Rather than portraying an event of the past, its "real and thoroughly effective action"[4] recaptures the event itself. Opposing a purely commemorative interpretation, Christian sacramentology has always insisted on the *real* effectiveness of its rites. The ritual becomes effective by creating a new temporality in which the successive attains permanence. Tearing itself loose from the coherent fabric of time-measured-by-space, it boldly reaches back to the aboriginal, "pure" experience of time.

Henri Bergson has shown that time, essentially a mental process, reluctantly submits to the homogeneous measuring of movement in space. The experience of internal duration incessantly resists its spatial projections. No experience of duration entirely resembles another. The mind grudgingly accepts the flattening homogenization of a "standard" time imposed by the bodily need to move around in a homogeneously spatial universe. Human beings internally resist this flatness and feel compelled to express duration in gestures that, though spatial themselves, nevertheless break through the *continuous* structure of the spatio-temporal. We know that a sacred place must be segregated from its surrounding space, that *templum* is derived from *temnein*. But spatial segregation is possible only because humans know how to express themselves in gestures of a different duration. Discontinuous with the preceding moment, the ritual deed is no longer subject to the transitoriness of common time. For that transitoriness, that defini-

4. Ernst Cassirer, *The Philosophy of Symbolic Forms* (New Haven: Yale University Press, 1955), 2:39.

tive irreversibility, is not inherent in the time structure as such, but results from its information in a homogeneous spatial system. Only in space does time become strictly one-dimensional. To be sure, time is always successive, but in ritual it ceases to be irreversibly successive. The lower we descend to cosmic homogeneity, the more time approaches the sheer contiguity and repetitiveness of parts in space. The higher we ascend to the pure experience of time, the more each unit differs from all others and the more freely we leap back and forth across the tightly cemented continuance of spatio-temporality. Here neither clock nor calendar measure duration, but rather the unifying awareness of a constancy underlying all succession. It is in that realm of recollection, of inward gathering, that ritual takes place.

The sacred deed recaptures the primeval time of a god, a hero, an ancestor. "Ritual abolishes profane, chronological time and recovers the sacred time of myth. Man becomes contemporary with the exploits that the gods performed *in illo tempore.*"[5] The noble simplicity of Mircea Eliade's wording may hide its amazing reality. With one stroke the privileged time of ritual reverses the direction of our ordinary sense of duration. The primordial assumption that certain times differ essentially from others lies at the root of the primeval assertion of transcendence. Not based solely on experience, that assertion emerges rather from a bold refusal to be satisfied with experience alone. Here also originates the awareness of immortality — time without end — which has played such a powerful role in the development of civilized life. Some have thought this belief to be grounded in the steady experience of the seasonal cycles, a constant sign that not all is lost when decay and death set in. But the religious calendar never coincides with the rhythms of nature.[6] The distinction between reversible (essential) and irreversible (contingent) time, while attempting to retain the meaningful moments in an essentially transitory life, also provides the most basic distinction needed for expressing a transcendent dimension in existence. What distinguishes sacred time is not that it remains present, but that it can be recalled from the past. The past has always been the gate to whatever permanence we may hope to acquire. The present constantly confronts us with the fleetingness of

5. Mircea Eliade, *The Myth of Eternal Return* (New York: Pantheon, 1954), p. 140.

6. H. Hubert and M. Mauss, *Mélanges d'histoire des religions* (Paris: La Renaissance du Livre, 1909), pp. 213ff.

an existence in time, while the past freezes the flux of becoming into definitiveness. For Plato, the eternal can only be *remembered,* while the Church Fathers refer to the awareness of God's presence as *memoria Dei.* Recollection alone gives access to what is no longer subject to change. In recapturing a privileged moment of the past, ritual reestablishes that permanence in the present.

Anthropologists and sociologists tend to consider religious ritual essential to life in society. Such was Durkheim's well-known thesis. It is undoubtedly true — in ritual individual and society interpenetrate one another. But at the same time, ritual transcends the merely social or, rather, in ritual the social *transcends itself.* It constitutes what Victor Turner has called the antistructure, the realm of the inner *communitas,* rather than the structure, the externally defined *societas.*[7] Ritual behavior never merely repeats the ordinary gestures of life. It formalizes and schematizes them until they become "different." The ritual mode of eating, drinking, walking, and dancing removes the act from the common performance. It bestows new meaning upon the ordinary. "Rites *symbolize* joyful and sad occasions, but never turn joyful or sad themselves. They express love without passion, austerity without hardship, sorrow without grief. Rites articulate real life, they mold it into their restrictive forms but they never fully merge with it."[8] As I still believe this paradox to be true, I consider attempts to bring the cult down to "everyday life" ill-directed and destructive of the metaphorical quality so essential to ritualization.

The rite derives its force precisely from the fact that it remains free of the ambiguity inherent in even the simplest deed. It presents the ideal deed, the one the gods themselves performed before the confusion of historical time. Having imitated the archaic gesture in its aboriginal purity, we are once again in a position to discover the pristine meaning of its daily use. But the model deed, because ideal, never becomes an integral part of that intricate net of half-formed intentions and incomplete gestures that relegate our daily course of action to permanent indefiniteness. In the field of ordinary activity the impact of our decisions is rarely manifest until long after the deeds have been performed. Before the act has been completed, the initial

7. Victor Turner: *Dramas, Fields and Metaphors* (Ithaca, N.Y.: Cornell University Press, 1974), pp. 52-53.

8. Louis Dupré, *The Other Dimension* (New York: Seabury Press, 1979), p. 128.

impulse has been caught in a web of uncontrollable contingencies that obfuscate its initial meaning. The duplicity may not be the agent's fault. His intentions may be simple and straightforward. But even if he knows his own mind and expresses it clearly in his action, the expressed intention itself allows no more than an ambiguous revelation. The outward gesture irresistibly moves away from the clear simplicity of intentions into the iron chain of causes and effects, countless and unpredictable. The ritual deed, in contrast, remains forever frozen in a temporality of its own, detached from historical time. Its definitiveness avoids the uncertainty of temporal events. Withdrawing from the world of action, it slows down to a contemplative ritardando, which elevates the deed to its ideal image. The rules are clearly established and the time is predetermined.[9]

Time in Ritual

But how can what moves in time redeem temporality? The answer, I suspect, lies in the different time conjuncture of ritual performances. Every act, every experience moves in its own time. But the time of ordinary acts merges with that of others, and together they constitute our common time experience. The rite resists such a synchronization. As an irreducible model that restores order against an ever-invading chaos, it has its foundation outside the ordinary succession of time — *in illo tempore*. The connection with a founding event is particularly strong in historical faiths. While in most religions the event itself lies buried in the mist of an unknown past, in Judaism and in Christianity rites represent a founding act performed at a specific moment of history. Often the faithful may not succeed in identifying that moment, but this has not prevented them from appealing to a unique event in the founding time, however dubious the link with that event may be.

Nor does the role of ritual become less important when those founding events as well as their meaning are lost in an irretrievable past. For without *re-presenting* primordial deeds, a religion evaporates into a purely interior attitude, in which salvation is remembered but not renewed. Through its rites, faith reactivates the sources of salvation. The

9. Cornelis Verhoeven, "Wat is een ritus?" in *Rondom de leegte* (Utrecht, The Netherlands: Ambo, 1965), pp. 9-49.

Eucharistic rite perpetuated Christ's oblation in death into a renewable sacrifice. Earlier in this century, Dom Odo Casel aroused a major controversy by his claims concerning the possibility of rendering past events ritually present. His opponents objected that the past cannot be recalled to the present. Such a principle of interpretation, if generalized, would undermine the fundamental doctrines of the Christian faith. Founding deeds are never *merely* historical. They transcend history in a way that enables them to reach men and women in all ages. It is precisely this permanent reality that the ritual *re-presents* to each new generation. To interpret rites, then, as mere commemorations is to miss their meaning. The Incarnation will remain significant to Christians only as long as the birth of Christ, both the eternal birth of the Son and the temporal birth of Jesus, continues to be recalled to an actual present. Such a reversal of time the Christmas liturgy implies when the choir at the opening of the Midnight Mass intones: *"Dominus dixit ad me: Filius meus es tu, ego* hodie *genui te"* — "The Lord spoke to me: *Today* I have begotten you." Similarly the Easter rite does not "commemorate" the resurrection of Christ: it *re-presents* it, year after year. In the words of the *Exultet:* "Haec *nox est, in qua destructis vinculis mortis, Christus ab inferis victor ascendit." "This* is the night in which Christ broke the chains of death and rose victorious from the nether world."

In the process of this ritual recall, history in its entirety acquires a different meaning. Historical facts are inextricably linked to other historical facts. In re-presenting one event, we inevitably evoke all others connected with it and, since the fabric of history is continuous all the way to the present, *all* events attain a new potential to be retrieved from the past. The representation of Christ's sacrificial deed co-presents all those whom his sacrificial death affected. This, as artists have always known, includes not only Christ's contemporaries, but men and women of all ages, before and after Christ. Benjamin Britten composed a Christian opera on the pre-Christian rape of Lucrecia, and Paul Claudel exclaimed in *La ville:*

Rien n'a pu ou ne peut
Être qui ne soit à ce moment même; toutes
Choses sont présentes pour moi.

Nothing has been or can be that is not in that very moment; all things are present for me.

In the Christian ritual, then, all of history becomes present. Its symbolism pledges that no part of the past is entirely lost.

Though oriented toward the past, ritual does more than repeat a gesture transmitted from time immemorial. A creative act in its own right, it constitutes meaning where none existed before. It is as new as it is old. Nor does ritual simply formalize the return of the seasons in nature. To be sure, it incorporates their rhythmic succession. But the seasons are not the primary signifiers, for they themselves receive their meaning through the ideal structure of the rite. Developed religions have never relied solely on natural periodizations and have consistently asserted the distinctness of their structuring symbols from the cycles of nature. Some, such as Judaism, Islam, and Mithraism, have detached the sacred times from their seasonal origins altogether.

The secularization of the modern age has radically changed our attitude toward ritual. Nature and time no longer hold the sacred meaning that our ancestors attributed to them. The general loss of the sacred as an integrating factor of life is too complex a phenomenon to be explained by a single cause. The objectivism of our worldview, grown steadily since the sixteenth century, has, of course, adversely affected the very possibility of transcending the closed circuit of spatialized, rectilinear time. Moreover, it has weakened our ability to conceive of any human activity as totally nonfunctional with respect to the ordinary course of life. The modern mentality undermines the inclination to take certain aspects of play-acting with absolute seriousness — as ritual practice requires. But perhaps more than any other single factor, the kind of historical awareness that has developed over the last two centuries has obstructed a correct understanding of ritual behavior. From the beginning Christians had insisted on the historical uniqueness of their faith: Christ was born under Tiberius and died under Pontius Pilate. Yet what emerged at the end of the eighteenth century was different. Beyond the uniqueness of historical events, educated Europeans for the first time began to consider events as segments of a continuous line from which they could never be detached. Not only could the same event never occur twice in its existential singularity: it was not even seriously comparable to any more recent event, since its very *essence* restricted it to an irreversible past. Integrated with a unique and all-comprehensive cultural totality, it remained unrepeatable and excluded any repetition in another epoch. While seventeenth-century literary critics could still argue about the greater significance of ancient or modern writers, the Romantics discovered the past as definitively completed and therefore unrepeatable. The ruins of Pompeii and the medieval castles of Scotland fascinated precisely because they were anachronistic witnesses of an irreversible past. With this new awareness of the past as past historians ceased to consult the past for moral lessons and instead started concentrating exclusively on the question of how, precisely, things had been. Earlier attempts to represent past events in a contemporary setting, so common in the Middle Ages and even long thereafter, now became themselves quaint relics of an unrepeatable past. With the possibility of recapturing the past thus challenged, the ritual intention to overcome time lost much of its meaning. The past was definitively closed, and only one dimension of time remained open: the future. The epoch that discovered history was also the first to shift the priority from the past to the future. Belief in progress and effective action to achieve it replaced the search for meaning in the past through remembrance and ritual repetition.

This epochal reversal of our orientation in time has created a major problem in our culture. One of the most unsettling aspects of modern life may well consist in a temporality conceived as being exclusively oriented toward the future. Unlike their ancestors, our Western contemporaries tend to view temporality as in principle subject to human control and life itself as a planned career. One critic of modernity spells out the disastrous effects of such an approach.

> There is no reason to doubt what battalions of psychologists have been telling us for decades, namely that the pace of modern living is detrimental to mental well-being and may also be harmful to physical health. Futurity means endless striving, restlessness, and a mounting incapacity for repose. It is precisely this aspect of modernization that is perceived as dehumanizing in many non-Western cultures. There have also been strong rebellions against it within Western societies — a good deal of both youth culture and counter-culture can, I think, be understood as insurrections against the tyranny of modern futurity.[10]

10. Peter Berger, *Facing up to Modernity* (New York: Basic Books, 1977), p. 74. Emile Durkheim made the same observation around the turn of the century when he described the modern individual's life as guided by "a restless movement, a planless . . . self-development, an aim of living which has no criterion of value and in which happiness lies always in the future, and never in any present achievement." *Le suicide*

We in North America have taken this turn toward the future more decisively than has any other society in the past or the present. "The American lives on the very edge of the now, always ready to leap toward the future" (Octavio Paz). Less known is the exceedingly high price we pay for living a life that consists primarily of promises. No place, no occupation, no relation provides the security of lastingness. Our activity remains mostly functional, directed by the goal to be obtained, rather than by intrinsic meaning. Everything bears the mark of transition. The result has been a pervading ugliness in our civilization and a lack of style on all levels of life. Even the churches tend to forget their own sacred gestures, often replacing the old rite by the bare, functional move, the venerable text by the practical language of everyday communication.[11] With the sense of a reversible past has vanished the sense of a meaningful present. It was the ritual's task to preserve both.

Secular Rituals

As no religious substitute for the meaning-giving role of ritual has been found in modern life, our contemporaries look for it in different, secular places: the sports arena and the theater. While doing so they unwittingly return to the ancient rites of the Olympian and Dionysian cults: games and drama. Yet for those who have lost religious innocence, the meaning and purpose of those ritual celebrations have undergone a drastic change: they have mostly ceased to relate the conflicts and tensions to the sacred powers of life and death. Even so, some measure of the cathartic impact that Aristotle attributed to the dramatic performance continues to exercise its salutary effect. Though modern playwrights and spectators no longer turn to the ancient rite for asserting their faith in the ultimate meaningfulness of the cosmic

(Paris, 1897), quoted in Erich Fromm, *The Sane Society* (New York: Holt, Rinehart, Winston, 1955), p. 191.

11. It was nevertheless Euripides who wrote the drama that most directly revived an ancient rite. Yet, as Jan Kott has observed, even in *The Bacchae,* two separate and contradictory structures exist — one sacred, the other profane. "Dionysus has been torn to pieces in *illo tempore,* in cosmic time; the dismemberment of Pentheus is carried into historic time, made visible in violent closeup." Jan Kott, *The Eating of the Gods* (New York: Random House, 1970), pp. 207, 220.

order and for exorcising the ever-encroaching forces of confusion and disorder, they do so implicitly by projecting their inner complexities upon the simplified (and in that sense ritualized) action of mythical agents. Even where drama achieves no more than expressing publicly the absence of meaning that spectators experience privately, it may still enable them to find at least some coherence for their lives in the unity of the play.[12] Yet acting no longer means partaking in a transcendent reality and thereby overcoming one's private contingency. Meaning, or the lack thereof, is thought to reside exclusively in the individual or in the closed group. Still in the abstract projection of psychological and social drama and in the simplified expression of absurdist theater something remains of the magic power inherent in the pure "acting" or ritual, so different from the "doing" or "making" that consumes most of our energy. In their unprecedented thirst for dramatic projection, our contemporaries continue to seek the "wholeness" that former ages sought in rite and ritual drama. A daytime television soap opera may have little else in common with the sophisticated production of a Shakespeare play, but both ritually project our concerns about the meaningfulness of life. As in other instances, literature attempts to substitute what the religious cult no longer provides for secularized men and women.

But drama may be more than a substitute. In drama the real action takes place in the spectators: the actors on the stage merely represent and articulate the conflicting drives that determine our existence. What induces human beings thus to put on masks of different personae? Does the need for an alien impersonation not originate in the quest for a more authentic self-expression? In some cases we identify more closely with our public role than in others. But we never succeed in doing so completely, and we constantly experiment with supplementary or alternative expressions. They may be no less artificial, but at least they differ from the persona expressed in our daily activities and relations in that we have freely chosen them. By joining a social club, a cultural organization, or any voluntary association, we assume parts that differ from the ones imposed by social traditions or professional functions. We call each other by

12. On the various dramatic traditions, see J. Chelsey Taylor and G. R. Thompson, eds., *Ritual, Realism and Revolt: Major Traditions in Drama* (New York: Scribner, 1972).

different names, observe particular conventions, and partake in deliberations concerning issues often too trivial to bother with in everyday life. But however devoid of intrinsic interest, these parts acquire a special significance simply by expressing the need to project ourselves beyond the ordinary.

In addition to those more or less durable parts, we still seek temporary respite from the "real" world in an occasional card or board game or an improvised match of softball. Even such recreational intermezzos engage us in the serious task of constantly reinventing the expression of an identity for which none of the roles of ordinary life suffice. In ordinary play, however, we refuse to commit our deeper self. One of the joys of playing consists precisely in not having to conform to any public or private image of ourselves. No normal person is able to view himself as "essentially" a poker player. Even the professional athlete is anxious to show that he or she is a fully human being with "deeper" concerns. Our identification with a self-chosen role becomes somewhat more intimate when we put on a mask — even for such frivolous purposes as a costumed carnival or a masked ball. Yet only in dramatic play do we perceive this impersonation itself as touching us below the surface. To be sure, most of the time spectators still maintain a safe distance between themselves and the often-threatening characters projected on the stage. The most sensitive actor still knows how to protect himself against a too hazardous identification. Nevertheless, in their multiple complexity and psychological subtlety, theatrical characters succeed in uncovering real qualities and tensions in ourselves that our common public and private appearances fail to reveal.

Drama allows us to take a temporary leave from the cares and joys of ordinary life, and language appropriately refers to such a stylized vacation as "play." Yet more than other forms of play, the images projected through theatrical alienation provide insight into the most private layers of our existence. The actor represents the kind of existential ambiguity we recognize in ourselves. In a complex way he links his own reality to the one he aesthetically projects. As Hans Urs von Balthasar put it, "His *displacement [Ver-stellung]* in the role serves the *re-presentation [Vor-stellung]* of that reality which only via displacement can enter the circle of the real. The actor appears as the medium in which two spheres of existence and truth encounter each other: the sphere of reality embodied in the public . . . and the sphere of our ideality, not directly attainable from within this reality, which the staged 'production' represents."[13]

The theater mysteriously merges the illusion of play with the deeper reality of life. Spectators identify with what they watch on the stage. They are aware of the distance between the actor and the character. Nevertheless they hold him or her responsible for the deeds he or she commits in that role. The stage forcefully reminds them both of their own need to project themselves in personae. Only in the *ek-stasis* of becoming what we are not does freedom allow us to become what we are. Watching the dramatic tensions in and among the staged characters, we realize that freedom demands that we "realize" ourselves within the confines of "character." Yet while doing so, we throw ourselves into an arena of tensions and struggles. The drama, then, unmistakably shows how the quest for identity leads through the alienation of role-acting.

From this perspective the ritual origin of drama reappears. Like ritual, drama possesses its own structured duration, separate from that indefinite passing of time in which moments merely succeed one another. Beginning, middle, and end of dramatic action impose an intensified and condensed temporality that has its own rhythmic alternations of tension and relaxation. Even as the rite, the drama occurs as an act in time, yet it surpasses time by its timeless disclosures. Though a paradigm of action in time, it surpasses the temporal transiency of the ordinary deed. Both in ritual and in drama, the developing action concludes in a state of affairs appropriate to the preceding events. Nevertheless, theatrical performance differs from liturgical ritual in that during the action the outcome remains unknown — even though the spectators persistently expect it to be an appropriate one. The drama never homogenizes the various parts that compose it, as ritual does. Conflicts may be resolved, but their resolution does not suspend the agonistic quality of existence itself. Participants in, and observers of ritual activity know from the start that all conflicts and tensions will be resolved. Though the outcome of the drama remains uncertain till the final act, the canonized form of dramatic processes assures the spectators that they may count on a definite, albeit not definitive, conclusion.

13. Hans Urs von Balthasar, *Theodramatik, vol. I, Prolegomena* (Einsiedeln, Switzerland: Johannes Verlag, 1973), p. 241.

At this point one may wonder how real life can draw comfort and enlightenment from such an artificial construction. Existence moves from one contingent occurrence to another, only to end in an often abrupt, always incomplete, conclusion. How, then, could it hope to derive meaning from a preconceived structure from which all non-sensical incoherence has been excised by the playwright and wherein irrationality is allowed to create only as much havoc as he or she tolerates? Despite such solid reasons against taking the drama seri-ously, we continue to attribute a paradigmatic quality to it — which includes the anticipated resolution of all struggles, however tragic. The playwright's own art anchors in the unspoken (and often con-sciously resisted) but fundamental belief that the dramatic struggle will result in some sort of harmony — often provisional, but symboli-cally anticipating a universal one — which surpasses what the *dramatic personae* themselves, within their internal and external conflicts, are able to achieve. Whatever the outcome of a good play, we never leave the theater without feeling that justice must and will be done — that no crime will remain unrevenged and no pain uncomforted. Nothing in the theatrical action justifies such a universal confidence, yet it lies at the root of drama itself. Irresistibly, we locate the staged succession of events within an all-comprehensive scheme of meaningful order. To that order reason has no access. Its credibility lies entirely in the acceptance of a higher standpoint, a transcendent judgment. Fate, or destiny, which plays such a decisive part in the classical tragedy and has been internalized but not eliminated in modern drama, articulates precisely this implicit belief. Rather than function as an unchangeable rule that renders all human efforts futile and reduces the tragedy to marionette play, it provides a perspective from which human actions receive meaning beyond the short-sighted intentions of their agents. Fate, destiny, or whatever ungraspable power continues to dominate modern drama signifies this superior presence that holds our acts accountable to a higher tribunal and assigns them bit parts in a wider, cosmic drama. Of this "play within a play" no one knows the final act except the overall director. Or, again in Balthasar's words, unso-licitedly man has been placed on the world podium.[14] This transcen-dent perspective on human destiny appears in the drama, which, without it, loses its meaning. For only from an implicit reference to

14. Balthasar, *Theodramatik*, I, pp. 10, 117.

a transcendent settlement of the conflict among the opposing claims made upon the person does the drama derive its ultimate meaningfulness. Drama, then, turns out to remain one of the major forms of religious ritual, not merely a substitute for it. Yet the modern attitude toward the transcendent, which refuses to name the unnameable, fiercely keeps this religious quality implicit.

Negative Theology
and Religious Symbols

That no predicates can be univocally attributed to God and the creature, is a principle on which all theologians agree. The issue which divides them is whether the negation of the inherently finite leaves room for an ultimate affirmation. Classical Hinduism and Buddhism have mostly denied that it does. Islam, Judaism and Christianity, on the contrary, have attempted to incorporate the negation within a new and definitive affirmation. Yet even here *apophatic* trends have always existed. In mystical writings the denial that positive attributes can be predicated of God reflects an actual inability to express a direct and intensive experience of the divine presence in positive language. In speculative theology the denial results as a logical conclusion from the presumed inadequacy of relative language to absolute Being. I shall concern myself primarily with the former, though the problems and solutions, if there be any, must in the end be identical in the two theologies. Their fundamental objection to any new affirmation, such as the one commonly implied in the analogy of Being, is that no qualification can ever overcome the inherent finitude of predicates which, by their very nature, are conceived for expressing the nature of a finite universe. When dealing with the Absolute one seldom reaches solutions by compromises.

Yet the objections against negative theology are equally formidable. Since negation alone never attains reality, either we inconsistently ascribe positive attributes to God, or we must settle for a total agnosticism. Such an agnosticism would jeopardize religious practice as much as religious theory: if God is totally unknown, prayer and

92

the entire religious attitude become meaningless. Man has nothing to
say to a God who remains beyond all determination. If we can assert
nothing *about* God, we can say nothing to Him — and that marks the
end of religion. It is a conclusion that not only mystics should ponder,
but also fideists — including those of the modern, Wittgensteinian
variety.

Negative theologians will reply that the attributes are negated, but
the ascending movement is not and, in fact, gains its momentum
precisely from the unceasing negation. This is true, but the movement
itself leads nowhere unless in the end *the negation itself be negated*. In
the following pages I shall attempt to show how such a final negation
entails in fact a new affirmation of the finite *within* the infinite and
consequently a new kind of analogy. Spinoza's philosophy here proves
to be particularly instructive. From the principle that determination
implies negation, the Dutch philosopher concludes that the absolute
substance must be beyond all determinations. But he should have
gone further and shown how the absolute nevertheless *includes* all
determination. Otherwise he is bound to find himself unable to introduce determination at all. It is only by an inconsistency that his
system realizes the transition from the infinite substance to the finite
modes. The same happens to negative theology: once its negative
movement reaches the One Absolute, it merely stops. Yet the Absolute
thus attained is an empty indeterminate, unable to justify the determinate being which supposedly proceeded from it and continues to
depend on it. A consistent negative theology reduces the creation (or
emanation) to an intrinsically unintelligible event and excludes the
possibility of any kind of revelation of the divine nature. It must be
admitted that some of the early Neoplatonist mystics appear to have
been satisfied with the affirmation of a dark void mysteriously present
to them in the spiritual experience. But, by and large, Christian mystics, even in the Neoplatonic tradition, have followed a different path.
Their God is essentially a *manifest* one even though none of our names
adequately describes him. After having declared God beyond predi-
cation, they perform an even more radical negation in a final attempt
to overcome human limitation altogether and to pass from the dark
of unknowing to the light of self-manifestation. Finding the finite
incommensurate to God's Being, the mystic ultimately abandons even
his right to judge the finite on his own (also finite) terms and asserts
its divine, immanent reality. He thus reaffirms the finite, not by

qualifying his original affirmation, but by radicalizing its negation so as to include negation itself and by allowing the divine affirmation to shine forth in its own right. The finite is reaffirmed as God asserts it in the identity of his own creative act, *not as it appears* in the opposition of its creaturehood.

> Divine transcendence ceases to mean negation of the creature, and instead becomes its elevation. Transcendence is no longer found *above* creation, but *in* creation. The creature is *in* God and God is *in* the creature. It is as *creature* and not only as uncreated essence that the creature manifests transcendence: God is the ultimate dimension of the finite reality, the inaccessible in the accessible.[1]

The concept of transcendence must itself be transcended and the final word about God is not absolute otherness but total identity. As George Morel admirably put it, "Man is not only creature, God is not only Creator."[2] It is this attitude which Ignatius of Loyola expresses in the last contemplation of his *Spiritual Exercises* when inviting the exercitant who previously has renounced all creatures for God to consider "how God dwells in creatures."[3] This negation of negation also determines the complex and seemingly contradictory dialectic of St. John of the Cross, which on one level denies all proportion between God and the creature, while on a different level asserting their full equality.[4] Even Eckhart, so strongly identified with the Neoplatonic tradition, does not conclude his ascent with the unknowable and merely negative One of Proclus and Pseudo-Dionysius. He does negate all *similarity* between God's *isness* and the creature's being, since likeness can exist only between the creature and God's *manifestation*, not between the manifest and the unmanifest one. Still his negation of all restricted being (and all being is restricted for Eckhart) ultimately results in a principle that includes all affirmations without excluding any one of them. Yet the presence of the ultimate in the finite does

---

1. Louis Dupré, *The Other Dimension* (New York: Doubleday, 1972), pp. 524-25.

2. *Le sens de l'existence d'après St. Jean de la Croix* (Paris: Aubier, 1960), Vol. II, p. 176.

3. *The Spiritual Exercises,* trans. Louis Puhl, S.J. (Westminister: Newman Press, 1954), p. 102.

4. For the former, cf. *Ascent of Mount Carmel* I, 6, 1; II, 8, 3; II, 12, 4; for the latter, *Spiritual Canticle* XV, 2 and numerous other passages.

not consist in a *likeness,* such as exists between cause and effect, but in the *identity* of being beneath the essential dissimilarity.

What in the analogy from the creature to God was "likeness" within dissimilarity becomes a sign of identity within distinctness in the analogy from God to the creature. In the latter analogy the degrees of perfection play no part. Eckhart writes: "God is neither good, better nor best." A recent interpreter comments: "It is not that God is *more* perfect; there is no 'more or less' in the All-inclusive."[5] Eckhart himself emphatically declares:

> Creatures [by themselves] are pure nothings. I do not say that they are either important or unimportant but that they are pure nothings. What has no isness [of and by itself] is nothing. Creatures have no isness of their own, for their isness is the presence of God.[6]

The infinite is present in the finite not through participative likeness but through identity of principle. The relation from the creature to God is not *ecstatic:* it is *instatic:* God contains all creatures within *his own* unity. Their difference from him is a merely negative characteristic, a mere limitation of their reality, not that reality itself. "By negating of God something that I assert that he is not — even this negation must go. God is One, he is the negation of negations."[7]

One might object that the preceding discards the well-established tradition of the creature, especially the soul, as image of God. But at the very origin of this tradition we find that the image itself was conceived, not as a likeness but as a presence of, and, ultimately, as an identity with God. To Origen the mind is the image of God precisely insofar as it is the place where the divine Logos resides, and it becomes more image as the presence increases. The sensible world presents only signs and shadows to be assumed *and overcome* by the mind. The Platonic ascent from bodily to spiritual knowledge is radically transformed by the immanent presence of the Divine Logos in the soul.

5. C. F. Kelley, *Meister Eckhart on Divine Knowledge* (New Haven: Yale University Press, 1977), p. 169. I borrow the expression "inverted analogy" from Kelley.

6. *Meister Eckhart. Die deutschen Werke,* ed. Joseph Quint, *et al.* (Stuttgart: Kohlhammer, 1938ff.), Vol. I, pp. 69-70. *Meister Eckhart: A Modern Translation* by Raymond Bernard Blakney (New York: Harper Brothers, 1941, [1957]), p. 185. I changed the term "Being" into "isness" to avoid confusion since Eckhart declares that God has no being. *Ibid.,* p. 219.

7. *Eckhart, Die deutschen Werke,* I, p. 364, trans. C. F. Kelley, *op. cit.,* p. 170.

While for Plato the Forms reside in the soul, for Origen and the Greek Fathers who adopted his theory of the image of God, the soul at some point actively coincides with the Eternal Logos.

> There is a certain affinity between the mind and God, of whom the mind is an intellectual image, and by reason of this fact the mind, especially if it is separated and purified from bodily matter, is able to have some perception of the divine nature.[8]

The mind resembles God, because it directly *partakes* in divine Nature. Likeness means dynamic presence of the Logos, not mere similarity of structure as in Cajetan's theory of analogy. The Alexandrian and Cappadocian Fathers knew both. But they singled out the image of the soul because only the soul reaches a conscious identity. Origen dismisses the similarity between God and the material universe as an inferior likeness. Later Eckhart was to refer to the knowledge of God through the creatures as "the cognition of the evening," in contrast to the matutinal knowledge of God and of the creatures in God. The soul's intrinsic participation in the divine appears even more explicitly in Gregory of Nyssa, who, with Augustine, gave the theory of the image its classical expression. To him that the soul is an image of God means that it directly partakes of a divine archetype.

> The eye enjoys the rays of light by virtue of the light which it has in itself by nature that it may apprehend the kindred light. . . . The same necessity requires, as regards the participation in God, that in the nature that is to enjoy God there be something kindred to him who is to be partaken of.[9]

Only because the soul partakes in the divine reality is it able to know God. The mystical life consists in turning more and more in toward "the image," that is, the presence of God in the soul. Significantly Gregory describes this presence as a dark cloud of unknowing, and thereby directly connects the image of God with the negative theology.

We detect a similar trend toward knowledge beyond images in St. Augustine. While in his early *De Quantitate Animae* Augustine attributes to all creatures a likeness of God though inferior to the one

8. Origen, *De Primis Principiis,* I, 1.7.
9. Gregory of Nyssa, *De Infant,* P.G. 46, 113D.

possessed by the soul, in the *Confessions* he emphasizes that the soul must turn into itself and leave behind not only all external creatures but even the faculties themselves. God dwells directly only in the soul and there is no proportion between his inner presence and the intimations of likeness in the creatures. The idea that only the mind is a true image of God gained power in the final period of Augustine's writing. In a treatise on contemplative life, the *Commentary on Psalm 41*, he expresses both the inadequacy of the creatures and the need to ascend beyond the self.

> For I see the things which my God has made and my God himself I do not see. . . . Having therefore sought to find my God in visible, bodily things and found Him not, having sought to find his substance in myself and found it not, I perceive my God to be higher than my soul. . . . I have poured forth my soul above myself. No longer is there any being for me to touch save my God.[10]

> In his own similitude let us seek God: in his own image recognize the Creator.[11]

The self as principle of transcendence must itself be transcended.[12] The soul is an image of God only to the extent that it is related to God, and it is related to God by participating in God.

> The true honor of man is the image and likeness of God, which is not preserved save in relation to Him by whom it is impressed. The less therefore he loves what is his own, the more he adheres to God.[13]

The more we know God, the more we love God and the more we become united with God. The practice of spiritual life consists not in seeing God in a pre-existing image but in becoming an image through

---

10. *Enarratio in psalmos,* Ps. 41, 7, P.L. 36, pp. 467-69, trans. by Elmer O'Brien in *Varieties of Mystic Experience* (New York: Holt, Rinehart, Winston, 1964), p. 68.

11. *In Johannis Evangelium,* XXIII, 10, P.L. 35, pp. 1588-89.

12. Augustine, *Sermones,* P.L. 38, p. 1457. In Sermon 330 Augustine writes: Return to thyself; but when, again facing upwards, thou hast returned to thyself, stay not in thyself. First return to thyself from the things that are without and then give thyself back to him that made thee.

13. Augustine, *De Trinitate* 12, 11, 16, P.L. 42, pp. 1006-7.

greater unity. "No creature, howsoever rational and intellectual, is lighted of itself, but is lighted by participation of Eternal Truth."[14]

Though religious mysticism always entails an intensive awareness of God's presence in creation, Christian mystics invariably commence their journey by emphasizing the difference (and hence the absence) between God and the creature. Their negative attitude must not be attributed only to practical wisdom but, first and foremost, to an immediate awareness that the creature as such is totally unlike God. For years Newman attempted to explain how through the phenomena of the visible world we gain "an image of God." But more and more he became convinced that only a previous awareness of God's inner presence — in conscience — would enable the mind to detect a divine presence in the world at all. In contrast to this "definite" presence in conscience "the phenomena are as if pictures, but at the same time they give us no exact measure or character of the unknown things beyond them."[15] The mind lacks the power to derive an image of God from the cause and system of the world.

> What strikes the mind so forcibly and so painfully, is His absence (if I may so speak) from His own world. It is a silence that speaks. It is as if others had got possession of His work. Why does not He, our Maker and Ruler, give us some immediate knowledge of Himself?[16]

In the moving sermon "Waiting for Christ" this alienation appears even more strongly.

> When he came in the flesh 'He was in the world, and the world was made by Him, and the world knew Him not.' Nor did He strive nor cry, nor lift up His voice in the streets. So it is now. He still is here; He still whispers to us, He still makes signs to us. But His voice is too low, and the world's din is so loud, and His signs are so covert, and the world is so restless, that it is difficult to determine when He addresses us, and what He says. Religious men cannot but feel, in various ways, that His providence is guiding them and blessing them personally on the whole; yet when they attempt to put their finger upon the times and places, the traces of His presence disappear. . . .[17]

14. *De Trinitate* 14, 14, 18, P.L. 42, 1049-50.

15. John Henry Newman, *A Grammar of Assent* (New York: Doubleday, 1958), p. 109.

16. *Ibid.,* p. 39.

17. *Parochial and Plain Sermons,* VI, p. 248.

Once again the inner presence must mediate the visible world with its Creator. Whatever divine clarity radiates from the creature is reflected back from the mind's internal light. In this light "things which come before our eyes, in such wise take the form of types and omens of things moral or future, that the spirit within us cannot but reach forward and presage what it is not told from what it sees."[18] The ambiguous signs of the visible world must await the interpretation of the inner voice. God remains "hidden" in a world that does not allow him "to display his glory openly."[19] Like Pascal, Newman concludes that without the "eyes of faith" the mind is unable to recognize God in his creation. Nor is this inner light derived from the mind's reflective powers. Even the voice of conscience becomes the voice of God only to him who knows how to listen to it as to a message originating beyond the self. We are reminded of Augustine's entreaty to move beyond memory and beyond the self.

The more the awareness of God's presence increases, the more the idea of a similarity between God and the creature recedes. The spiritual soul does not look for "God-resembling" creatures. It embraces all beings with equal fervor. Perceiving the divine presence as much in the lowly as in the high, in the bad as in the good, it abandons its preferences for the good and the beautiful in order to seek out an identical presence underneath opposite appearances. Symbols of creation are not analogues of divine attributes: the singing of the nightingale comes no closer to God than the croaking of the frog. Still the absence of picture-likeness does not reduce religious symbols to the status of arbitrary signs. The relation between the religious sign and the divine Signified surpasses in intimacy the one between a picture and its model. For the reality disclosed by the symbol is not an extrinsic one, but *its own:* the finite *intrinsically* participates in the Infinite. Its *specific* nature reveals only God's *outward* (i.e., nonidentical) manifestation, not his intimate Being.

Nor does it follow that all creatures are virtually identical as symbols of the Transcendent. The insurmountable difference between their essential being and the divine reality in no way prevents them from *disclosing* its presence in various and even unequal modes.

18. *Ibid.,* p. 249.

19. "The Omnipotence of God the Reason for Faith and Hope," in *Parochial and Plain Sermons.*

Hence the particular predisposition of some to become "religious" symbols proper. But this inequality depends on *the mind's particular openness* to certain signs rather than to others, not on the greater similarity of the disclosing symbols to the divine. Their hierarchy constitutes an anthropological order. Not because their signifying power is purely subjective; that power is real and objective, but it resides in a particular ability to *disclose* a transcendent presence, not in a presumed similarity with that reality. The contrary position makes it hard to understand why a creature of a lower type — e.g., an animal, or a stone — is selected to symbolize the divine in preference to one of a higher type. Symbols favored for their religious significance — such as light, mountains, etc. — are by no means the highest in the hierarchy of being. Even humans owe their unique status as religious symbol not so much to their elevated rank in being as to their singular *awareness* of the divine presence both in themselves and in other beings. To the person alone God is present, because he alone lives in a *present*. As the sole interpreter of that presence, he alone mediates the creation with God through his awareness of a divine immanence. Hence the most prominent symbol of the divine has always been the man or woman most intensively aware of its presence.

The thesis argued in the preceding pages should be well distinguished from the position of negative theology and of dialectical theology. Far from denying religious symbols their significant power, I argue that this significance is one of *presence* rather than of similitude. I fully accept not only the possibility of genuinely religious symbols, but even their necessity. Without symbols no religious experience at all could occur, since the experience originates *in* and *through* the symbols. Nor does the power of symbols derive exclusively from individual or communal decisions to single out certain phenomena for special significance. It is true enough that in the major faiths of the West an authoritative "revelation" establishes both the leading symbols and the determining symbolic structures. But such an institution could not take place if the religious mind were not *by its very nature* symbolic, and selectively so. Even the symbols of a revealed religion do not owe their entire power to the authority of that revelation, but, in an equal measure, to an inherent religious expressiveness. Symbols do not signify because they are thought to be revealed, but they are selected to reveal because they are endowed with a natural significance. Previous to any revelation there exists a religious receptiveness in the mind's very perception of the phenomenal world. To say this is not to minimize the creative impact of the revelatory event, but merely to assert that its structuring and specifying activity is conditioned by the religious symbolizing function of the mind itself.

This conclusion, of course, leaves us with the question: How do phenomena symbolize the divine? It is a question on which the phenomenology of religion has already spent much attention, yet for which it has found no satisfactory answer. Yet this much seems clear. The religious mind selects its symbols according to the power of natural phenomena to convey a sense of extraordinary *presence*. Theories of the religious experience, from the early "dynamic" ones to Eliade's "ontic" one, all insist on this awareness of presence. Identical symbols appear in totally unrelated religions because, beyond their specific significations, they are able to manifest a divine presence. Thus phenomena that abruptly distinguish themselves from the ordinary, the high mountain peak, the loud thunderclap, the sudden clearing and, everywhere, the brilliant light, all convey a sense of immediate presence more than they evoke a specific feeling.

In this respect, however, the modern attitude differs substantially from that of previous epochs. In the first place because the empiricist attitude, dominant in modern life, tends to oppose the symbolic to the real. Events and words are perceived as *either* symbolic *or* real (in an exclusively literal or observational sense). Such a disjunction causes problems for understanding religious symbols, particularly in a historical faith such as Christianity. It drains the paradigmatic events of faith from their enduring significance and encourages a strictly factual, historical interpretation of Scripture. As a result, sacramental deeds or words, which both partake of the ordinary, historical world and yet signify a deeper, hidden reality, have lost much of their meaning for our contemporaries. These epistemic problems in the understanding of religious symbols come, of course, in addition to the more fundamental one that the populations of Western Europe and, to a lesser extent, of North America have become essentially secular in outlook. Nature, to them, rarely reveals a divine presence. If God still speaks, he seldom does so through the voice of nature. Nor are they much disposed toward creating new symbols for what to many is no longer a living reality.

The loss of perceptiveness for religious symbols, however, does not mean that the sense of the symbolic has disappeared altogether.

The opposite is the case. I doubt whether any previous age has seen a more powerful explosion of symbolic creativity as we witness today. The artistic expansion in all directions resembles the "big bang" of creation. *Precisely because* symbolic creativity has become increasingly detached from an established, given order of reality, has it been able to take such an uninhibited flight. Our artistic symbols create autonomous orders of their own. Georg Lukacs has argued (rightly, I think) that the disappearance of a meaning inherent in existence accounts for the growth of the modern novel. Fiction recovers a meaning that we no longer consider to be given with reality itself. Thus Michel Foucault regarded *Don Quixote* the first modern work of literature, "because in it language breaks off its old kinship with things and enters into that lonely sovereignty from which it will reappear, in a separated state, only as literature."[20] Yet as writers and artists freed themselves more and more from the given order of things they also increasingly came to realize that the patterns of meaning so created remained primarily their own. Art and literature have assumed a private, often esoteric character. Works of art increasingly tend to become independent symbolic systems in their own right. Each symbolic structure (literary, artistic, social, political) projects itself as a fragmentary universe that has to compete with other "miniverses."

The boundless creativity of our age has made modern culture an exciting spectacle. Yet its symbols and symbolic structures no longer serve the function they served in the past, namely, to illuminate our journey through time. Symbolic structures created at random cease to provide guidance and turn into games. We find ourselves left with Eliot's "heap of broken images."

The picture I have painted of modern culture's loss of religious perceptiveness may seem bleak, yet it is not hopeless. Has the religious mind not always experienced difficulty (though perhaps not as acutely as today) in attempting to render the invisible visible? Were it not just the most intensely religious men and women who ended up declaring all names of God to be inadequate? Significantly, mystics in East and West have consistently been the strongest advocates of a negative theology. The atheism of our culture may have placed all believers in a condition where they, religiously underprivileged, are forced to learn

---

20. Michel Foucault, *The Order of Things* (New York: Vintage Books, 1973), pp. 48-49).

from those who were spiritually most endowed that no *natural* symbols will ever be adequate for thinking and speaking of God. This is not to say that the religious mind may dispense with symbols altogether. Dionysius himself, the Christian father of negative theology, wrote a treatise on the need for divine names. Without metaphors and analogies humans can neither think nor speak, least of all about the unnamable. Any attempt to bypass religious symbols can only land the believer into the bogs of subjectivism.

The more subtle conclusion to draw from our situation is that no single symbol is qualified, at the exclusion of others, to refer to a transcendence that is both hidden and omnipresent. In the past saints reached that conclusion at the end of their spiritual journey. We, confronted with a world in which nothing *appears* God-like, are forced to assume it from the start. Nor does it imply that all symbols have become equal. Some undoubtedly lend themselves more readily to the language of mystery than others, because they appear more noble, or more remote from the ordinary view of things, or for any other reason that causes them to provoke reflection. Yet none can claim an intrinsic or exclusive quality of holiness. Today the analogy of Being, so persistently defended by Christian, especially Catholic, theology, ought to begin with the "katalogy" of the mystics, the analogy that starts from above, that is, from the revelation of a divine mystery, rather than from a presumed knowledge of what God must be like on the basis of creation. It probably also ought to be an analogy of the imagination more than of the understanding.[21] A confrontation with the divine mystery evokes the imagination's creative power before it settles down on the reflective conceptualization of mystery.

21. David Tracy, *The Analogical Imagination* (New York: Crossroad, 1989).

PART III

Religious Experience

Experience and Interpretation: A Philosophical Reflection on Schillebeeckx's Theology

In an age when religion can no longer count on the support of the entire culture, the emphasis on experience becomes essential for its survival. To perceive the meaning of religion one must, even in the midst of one's secular experience, find intimations of a transcendent mystery. In turning to a revealed religion this tends to shift the weight from the message to the experience of those who received it, both the original ones and their successors today. Such a shift in emphasis creates a host of hermeneutical problems. To mention only one: How can a historical figure, living in a remote culture, initiate a universal experience and even elicit new experiences at a time that has become fully estranged from the religious culture in which the message was delivered? The theologian Edward Schillebeeckx squarely confronts that problem in two major studies, translated into English as *Jesus* and *Christ*.

For him, Christ's message is not a clearly formulated assertion, but rather "a catalyzing question, an invitation."[1] The defining significance of Jesus' presence lies in the individual and social responses to that question. The response to the message affects the entire experience of the respondents — now as in the past. "What speaks to us in Jesus is his being human, and thereby opening up to us the deepest possibilities from our own life, and in this God is expressed. The

---

1. Edward Schillebeeckx, *Jesus,* trans. Hubert Hoskins (New York: Seabury Press, 1979), p. 636.

divine revelation as accomplished in Jesus directs us to the mystery of man. Therefore to ask people to accept the Christian revelation before they have learnt to experience it as a definition of their own life is an impossible and useless demand."[2]

Schillebeeckx meticulously investigates how eyewitnesses and early Christians originally experienced Jesus' deeds and words in order to find out which experience, if any, they could possibly elicit in a culture that so strongly stresses its difference from the past. If there is an experience of grace in Christ, then all aspects of human experience will be affected by it, since all are continuous. To what extent can such a claim still be made in our contemporary world? Schillebeeckx is unambiguous on this point: only a Christology that extends to all aspects of the secular experience can develop the full cosmic implications of such New Testament writings as Colossians, Ephesians, and Hebrews, in which the Christ appears as the center of history and, ultimately, of creation.

The emphasis on experience need not be at the expense of historical objectivity, however. In contrast to the Bultmannian trend to abandon a hopeless search for the original historical facts in favor of their subjective reverberation in the primitive community, Schillebeeckx rejects the disjunction: *either* existential impact *or* historical objectivity. "My concern is indeed to hold a *fides quaerens intellectum* and an *intellectus quaerens fidem* together."[3] The experiences reflected in the New Testament were by their very nature intentional, that is, they noematically refer to the events that set them off and, hence, report an objective as well as a subjective reality. They require that we follow historical-critical as well as social-literary methods. But contrary to the traditional approach, the search for historical objectivity is only part of an overall attempt to recover the entire experience, objective as well as subjective.

We may summarize Schillebeeckx's theory as it is applied in his work and articulated in the *Interim Report* in the following two theses:

First, revelation can be received only in and through human experience. "There is no revelation without experience."[4] "The ex-

2. Edward Schillebeeckx, *Christ: The Experience of Jesus as Lord,* trans. John Bowden (New York: Seabury Press, 1980), p. 76.

3. Schillebeeckx, *Jesus,* p. 33.

4. Edward Schillebeeckx, *Interim Report on the Books Jesus and Christ,* trans. John Bowden (New York: Crossroads, 1981) p. 11.

perience is an essential part of the concept of revelation."[5] A harder formulation of this first thesis states: "Christianity is not a message which has to be believed, but an experience of faith that becomes a message."[6] Clearly, the two claims are not identical. According to one, the Christ revelation is conveyed *within* an experience; according to the other, Christianity *is* primarily experience. In both readings the term "experience" stresses the central place of a subjective element in revelation — either in its reception or in its constitution. Yet Schillebeeckx keeps a safe distance from a romantic concept of religion such as is found in Schleiermacher's *Discourses*. "The self-revelation of God does not manifest itself *from* [better translation, "on the basis of"] our experiences but in them."[7]

The second thesis differentiates Schillebeeckx's "experience" even further from romantic feeling. All experience contains elements of interpretation, not only in the subsequent reflection but already in the experiencing act itself.[8] With this second thesis the hermeneutical problem confronts us with full force, for at least part of this interpretation goes back to whatever cultural attitudes and religious expectations existed at the time of the experience. These extrinsic factors structured the experience in a particular conceptual apparatus and provided its models of interpretation. Nor do they enter experience at a later stage of reflection; they fuse with it from the start. "It is an obvious fact that they [the first Christians] made use of existing concepts like Messiah, son of man, and so forth, which have their own distinctive meaning — a historical accretion that was not in all respects applicable to Jesus: obvious too that understanding Jesus as they did to be the very essence of final salvation, they deliberately modified these concepts in the very act of applying them to Jesus."[9]

Now an experience couched in this kind of interpretation is no longer directly accessible to our contemporaries, who live by altogether different presuppositions, ideologies, and worldviews. Hence a first condition for the New Testament message of salvation to provide "inspiration and orientation" today is that we become aware

5. Schillebeeckx, *Report*, p. 12.
6. Schillebeeckx, *Report*, p. 50.
7. Schillebeeckx, *Report*, p. 12.
8. Cf. Schillebeeckx, *Report*, p. 13.
9. Schillebeeckx, *Jesus*, p. 50.

of its cultural assumptions. Schillebeeckx has devoted the greater part of his work to this seemingly simple but in fact never-ending task. But above all he has reformulated the old problem: How can the original, interpreted experience elicit a new experience of salvation in the present? Clearly there must be a causal connection between the first, privileged experience and all later ones. At the same time, the present experience must be genuinely new, since the elements of interpretation, integral parts of the experience itself, have changed.

The question of how an authoritative text can be transferred to a new realm of experience has emerged before in biblical criticism — with rather disastrous results. Lessing denied any definitive authority to a historical text. The principle that led him to this denial may appear naively rationalistic: contingent historical truths, that is, accounts of past events or experiences, can never form an adequate basis for the unchanging, necessary truths of reason. It may seem a confused one as well, for, as he develops his Enlightenment thesis, Lessing blends it with the altogether different one of the inadequacy of historical evidence, which in his view never suffices to support the kind of absolute commitment that faith requires. As Lessing formulates it, the first thesis is not likely to disturb the modern believer, who tends to hold a more restricted view of necessary truths than that of the rationalist Enlightenment, and who feels less inclined to separate historical from other truths. But underneath Lessing's first thesis lurks the deeper problem: How can the historically conditioned truth of one generation be the basis for that of another generation? And underneath the second: How can the immediate evidence of the eyewitness ever be transmitted to a later generation? Schillebeeckx fuses the two theses into one when he writes: "Lessing stresses 'rational experiential evidence' or 'immediate experiential evidence.' In that sense he interprets the Enlightenment's distinction between 'contingent truths' and 'necessary truths of reason.' What were necessary truths 'in the past,' become now, for the developed intellect which apprehends for itself, the intrinsic evidence of what 'religion' is, 'contingent truth.' "[10]

10. Schillebeeckx, *Jesus,* p. 584. This is clearly not what Lessing wrote, since a historical event never has the necessity of a *vérité de raison,* even for the eyewitness, the only epistemological necessity Lessing recognizes, although it may be indispensable for the discovery of a necessary truth. Schillebeeckx's interpretation, however, points to at least one thing Lessing meant: the absence or immediate compelling evidence in later generations.

Schillebeeckx takes up Lessing's problem again. First, however, he liberates it from its underlying antihistorical universalism. To reduce the essential content of Christianity to that of an "eternal truth" is to betray it altogether. There is an essential link between the historical person of Jesus and the religious message of absolute values he conveyed: Christian "truth" is intrinsically connected with Jesus' person. Without Jesus' Abba experience the Christian could nurture no hope in immortality or even in a better future or a meaningful development of history.[11] The Christian fruit cannot be severed from its historical tree. In a very real sense the fruit *is* the tree itself. Hence Schillebeeckx rejects not only Lessing's historical occasionalism (Christianity merely educated the human race to the discovery of what are essentially self-evident truths of reason) but any theory according to which the role of the historical Jesus is reduced to that of a catalyst for the discovery of wholly new and independent religious experiences.[12] For Schillebeeckx, the historical core at the heart of the original experience must be preserved in all later experiences. But how much of that core was saved in the edited reports of the New Testament? After all, the original core lies buried in ideologies, presuppositions, and worldviews from which no amount of scriptural detective work can fully liberate it. To what extent, then, must the transmitted text form the basis of our experience?

Schillebeeckx does not explicitly answer this question, but both his treatment of the text and his manner of defining guidelines for the new experience imply a response. Since the question is directly related to Lessing's problem, it may be instructive to return to the original discussion before evaluating the new answer. In his famous polemic with the Hamburg pastor Goeze, Lessing defended the "internal truth" of Christian revelation against the external authority of the text. "The scriptural traditions must be explained from the internal truth of religion, and no scriptural traditions can give it any internal truth if it have none."[13] Goeze pointedly replied that the term "internal truth" provides no criterion for distinguishing one text from

11. Schillebeeckx, *Jesus,* p. 270.
12. Schillebeeckx, *Jesus,* p. 586.
13. *Axiomata* 10. *Axiomata* (1978) forms part of Lessing's polemics with the Lutheran Pastor Goeze.

another, nor, we might add, one experience from another.[14] The
nature of revealed truth postulates, he felt, some authority to establish
it as revealed. When we deal with a codified revelation, as in Christianity, only some kind of recognition of the ultimate authority of
Scripture can secure its revealed nature. In Goeze's words, "Whoever
would explain to me the scriptural traditions from the internal truth
of religion must first convince me that he himself has a well-grounded
conception of the internal truth of the same, and that he does not
form for himself an image of it which suits his views."[15] Before being
in a position to argue the significance of the text, one must accept the
text as an authoritative source of truth. This excludes the attitude of
reading the Bible "as you read Livy," as Lessing suggested in the
Vindication of the Ineptus Religiosus.

Unlike Lessing, Schillebeeckx does accept the a priori authority
of the text and clearly rejects the ahistorical rationalistic universalism
of the Enlightenment, which still lingers on in our own day.[16] And
yet he would not be entirely on Goeze's side. After having traced each
pericope and verse to its proper layer of tradition (Q, pre-Marcan,
Marcan, etc.) the question returns: Now that we have exposed the
historical models, presuppositions, and ideologies that enter into the
composition of a New Testament passage, how does the text remain
decisively significant for the Christian today? If experience continues
to belong to the essence of revelation, the revealed message can have
practical authority only insofar as it still "inspires" today. The reader
then is to decide what in Scripture (whose authority he has accepted
in abstracto) still elicits a Christ experience and what not. Now this
may well describe the practice that Christians have followed for some
time, though usually with an uneasy conscience. The apocalyptic
passage in Jude 9 of the archangel Michael fighting with the devil over
Moses' body has long ceased to inspire the faithful. It puzzles them
and, to the extent that they attribute an absolute authority to each
single passage of Scripture, it disturbs them. Schillebeeckx effectively
shows how this piece of Hellenistic-Jewish lore was part of the com-

14. Kierkegaard struggled with this problem in *The Book on Adler: On Authority
and Revelation,* and also, with respect to the subjective nature of existential truth, in
The Unscientific Postscript.

15. *Axiomata* 10.

16. Schillebeeckx, *Jesus,* pp. 591-92.

mon religious culture in and through which Hellenistic-Jewish Christians interpreted their experience of salvation. Our own Christ experience passes through altogether different channels of interpretation. Since in the end the experience is decisive, the inaccessibility of an obsolete cultural interpretation should create no major difficulties.

But does this dispose of the whole problem? Must, at least to later generations, the original expression not remain as authoritative as the original experience? More precisely, can that experience itself ever be authoritative except through the expression? We cannot compare our experience with the original experience as if the two were on an even footing. The experience of those who lived at a time when the original impact of Jesus' appearance was still alive was in a unique way privileged. Yet that original experience reaches us exclusively through Scripture. Scriptural expression, then, must remain the final authoritative basis of our own experience. In this respect our experience essentially differs from the original one, since it occurs on the basis of an earlier, expressed experience. Here, then, lies at least an initial answer to the question explicitly raised in the *Interim Report:* "How far can this account [of the New Testament writers] of their experience of salvation in Jesus with its personal and collective coloring, still inspire us now and be our guide? And as Christians are we bound by all the interpretative elements?"[17] Since it is the expressed experience of the early communities that lies at the origin of our own, and since this expression indissolubly combines experience and interpretation, the entire New Testament text retains a unique authority. In order to continue in time, the revelation required some sort of definitive expression of the original, interpreted experience. Any attempt to separate the experience from the interpretation in this expression must run aground on Schillebeeckx' own solid principle of their indissoluble unity.

Nevertheless, it is equally certain that some elements of this expressed interpretation have become virtually unintelligible and have thereby lost at least the practical authority to determine our own Christ experience. Some distinction between experience and interpretation, then, must be made. But what are the criteria for such a distinction? Most educated Christians today do not blink an eye when hearing a good deal of the infancy pericopes in Luke and Matthew as well as a

17. Schillebeeckx, *Report,* p. 15.

number of sayings and events of Jesus' public life attributed to Judaic or Hellenistic narrative models rather than to historical facts. Yet theologians remain (rightly) reluctant to give a similar interpretation to the resurrection stories, even though they subject them to the same historical criticism. What in the New Testament reports should continue to determine authoritatively the modern experience to secure an essential continuity with the original experience, and what may safely be considered to belong exclusively to contemporary interpretation? Let us return to the section in *Jesus* on the resurrection.

Schillebeeckx distinguishes the Easter experience from the "articulation factor," which interprets this experience against a given horizon of understanding. "After his death Jesus himself stands at the source of what we are calling the 'Easter experience' of the disciples; at all events, what we meet with here is an experience of grace. But *qua* human experience it is self-cognizant and spontaneously allied with a particular expression of itself."[18] The author rightly dismisses the charge of pure subjectivism. He specifically repudiates the thesis that "resurrection and belief in the resurrection are one and the same thing."[19] The Easter experience, as he conceives it, is obviously more than a subjective state of consciousness, though we may not be able to point out today in what precisely its objective element consisted. As for the traditional expression of the experience in the stories of the empty tomb and the appearances, he hastens to add that that expression became in some way an intrinsic part of the total experience. Yet he distinguishes the original experience, which was directly caused by Christ, from its interpreted expression in the stories of the empty tomb and the appearances.[20] The Easter experience itself, as distinct from its linguistic interpretation, rests partly on the disciples' earlier acquaintance with the earthly Jesus and partly on a wholly new conversion process. This new experience does not "consist in experiences of an empty tomb or of 'appearances' (themselves already an interpretation of the resurrection faith)," but in "an encounter with grace" after Jesus' death.[21] The *Interim Report* restates the distinction in even clearer terms: "The visual element in what the Easter experience was

18. Schillebeeckx, *Jesus,* p. 392.
19. Schillebeeckx, *Jesus,* p. 644.
20. Schillebeeckx, *Jesus,* p. 393.
21. Schillebeeckx, *Jesus,* p. 394.

gains an evocative significance as a redundancy element when one stresses the cognitive aspect in the process of conversion which is implied in the names given by Christians to Jesus."[22]

On the basis of this clear distinction (though not separation) between the Easter experience and its interpreted expression, we should reconsider the question why Christians could not draw the same conclusion in this as in all other cases. Why should they in this one instance not be allowed to relativize the interpreted expression as culturally determined by models that are no longer available to them? To be sure, the expression "is an intrinsic aspect of the experience itself."[23] But in other cases this actual unity never constituted a sufficient basis for compelling the modern Christian to take experience and interpreted expression *per modum unius*. It invited him to seek *through* the interpreted expression the original experience and to expose himself to it in his own cultural context. As far as I can see, Schillebeeckx provides no clear criterion that would establish a unique connection of the Easter experience with its culture-bound expression. *Either* the salvation experience can be relived in forms that are not essentially bound to all the cultural models of the New Testament world (even though we become acquainted only through these models of interpretation), and then modern Christians could undergo the Easter experience while reserving judgment on the stories of the empty tomb and the appearances. *Or* the salvation experience and its New Testament expression are so indissolubly united that any attempt to regain that experience independent of its original models of expression becomes impossible or hazardous, and then each single element of the New Testament expression, however time-conditioned, retains

---

22. Schillebeeckx, *Report*, p. 81. Schillebeeckx admits that the exegete Descamps, in his favorable review of *Jesus*, gives the visual aspect "a more precise place . . . within the whole of what I call the process of conversion" (*Report*, p. 82). I wonder whether the term "central" would not have been more appropriate than "precise" for characterizing a position according to which the Easter experience cannot exist without those precise objective elements which we know through the resurrection narratives. He concedes fairly that "the visionary element is the one which the written texts present to us directly, whereas the hypothesis of the process of conversion — which is also cognitive — is simply a deduction, and cannot be directly recognized in the original scriptural texts" (*Report*, p. 82). Descamps's tighter connection between the experience and the events reported in the Gospel is based on a somewhat different evaluation of the significance of the narratives.

23. Schillebeeckx, *Jesus*, p. 392.

its full, effective authority in structuring the modern Christ experience. Both alternatives entail difficulties: relativizing the canonical text may jeopardize the continuity of experience, while giving it priority over the living experience may return us to biblical literalism.

The problem may perhaps be advanced by incorporating Schillebeeckx's valuable distinction between experience and interpretation into a more comprehensive, evolutionary understanding of revelation. He appears to grant the original experience a priority over the culturally conditioned elements of interpretation. Thus he ascribes only the Easter experience itself to Jesus as to its direct cause. There is, indeed, no doubt that experience precedes the subsequent reflective interpretation, and even that it enjoys an ontological (though not a temporal) priority with respect to that indispensable interpretation which gives structure, emphasis, and meaning to the primary experience. But there is still a third form of interpretation, which consists in the very possibility of experience and which, in the case of a transcendent revelation, must be given with the experience itself. Cultural elements may prepare humans for expressing a new experience of the transcendent in preexisting models and concepts, but nothing prepares or disposes us for the experience itself. This possibility contains the most basic interpretation, the fundamental orientation which urges it to choose some cultural models and exclude others and which guides the whole process of expression. This *primary interpretation,* consisting in the very possibility of a revelation, enjoys equal status with the original experience itself. To reduce it to a level below the experience is to perform an impossible abstraction on the experience itself. As a primary interpretation, it must be distinguished from the cultural interpretation through models and concepts. Since it conditions the very possibility of a revelatory experience, the primary interpretation cannot be detached from that experience. It forms no part of the process of expression as such, but directs it, determining which cultural models will be adopted and which ones will be rejected.

Schillebeeckx's strong assertion that the revelation is not a message but "an experience that became a message"[24] takes, in my opinion, insufficient account of this given, fundamental interpretation. Since it has also found its way into the New Testament expression, revelation is intrinsically, not secondarily, a universe of discourse, divine

24. Schillebeeckx, *Report,* p. 51.

expression, and hence message. The position I propose retains Schille-beeckx's basic insight that revelation is experience, but it qualifies his occasional emphasis of experience over expression. Those forms of interpretative expression which he discusses — the models, concepts, ideologies, expectations — belong, indeed, to the structuring rather than to the receiving of the actual experience. But the original core of revelation consists of both the experience and its given possibility, that is, its interpretative orientation. This given, primary interpretation enjoys the same privileged status as the experience itself, since it forms an essential part of it.

The original unity between experience and primary, expressed interpretation entails no need for a literalist reading of Scripture, for the original revelation event (I prefer this term, which denotes the objective as well as the subjective element) is from the beginning both totally culturally conditioned and God-given. Experience itself is by its very nature immanently human, and hence as much historically conditioned as its structuring and reflective interpretations. The aesthetic experience of nature did not emerge until the Hellenistic period, and the feeling of its sublime awesomeness not until the modern age. In both of these cases, as in all others, the experience was as conditioned as its interpretation. On a fundamental level, interpretation and experience are one. Somewhat analogously, in a revelation experience both primary experience and primary interpretation exist as a single, original unity. Hence the link with both must be preserved in later confrontations with the original Christ event. But at the same time both experience and interpretation develop — and this is what makes the hermeneutic enterprise so complex. Schillebeeckx's masterly analysis of the various levels of revelation has given it a new direction. Yet, instead of a single, privileged Jesus experience at the beginning, I would rather posit a continuing process of interpreted experience, of which with respect to later generations the first stage was not completed until it was codified, long after most eyewitnesses had died, in what later became the canonical text. The process would constantly pass through new experiences and interpretations, all of which, however, remain both subjectively and objectively dependent upon the original, interpreted experience.

The Experience of Mystical
Union in Western Religion

The term "mysticism" possesses many meanings, most of them vague and ill-defined. Some meanings restrict the mystical to exceptional religious states; others are comprehensive enough to include mental conditions neither exceptional nor religious. The present chapter focuses exclusively on exceptional religious experiences within monotheist faiths. Those experiences have a great deal in common from one faith to another — even outside monotheism. Does this imply, as some claim, that only doctrinal interpretations extrinsic to the experience distinguish similar mystical states from each other? Unquestionably each mystic tends to interpret his or her experience in the light of the theological or philosophical universe to which he or she belongs. Moreover, the nature of the spiritual quest determines the interpretation we give to its outcome. But to conclude therefrom that the interpretation remains extrinsic, amounts to denying the experience a specific, ideal content and reduces it to a purely subjective feeling. As William James showed long ago, the mystical experience is distinctly cognitive and intentionally unique.

It would, of course, fly in the face of what we know about mystical experiences to deny on the basis of theological prejudices that they display a family resemblance. It is in fact this resemblance which enables us to rank a variety of phenomena under some universal categories — as we do when we apply the general term "mysticism" to a number of experiences occurring in different religious contexts. The three monotheist religions of the West started with powerful personal experiences of their founders. I would add that all religions, regardless of their origin, retain their vitality only as long as their members retain some direct experience of transcendence. The significance religious traditions attach to those experiences varies from one religion to another. Monotheist religions tend to consider them less significant than do Vedantic Hinduism or some forms of Mahayana Buddhism. Nevertheless some experience, whether of higher or lower intensity, belongs to the essence of religion, and in that large sense at least we may claim that all religions have a mystical core.

Now, the mystical experience in the narrow, exceptional sense presents a unique challenge to the outsider who attempts to describe it. How do we know another person's experience? A study of mysticism is bound by the limits of expression and, if it deals with past mystics, by the limits of written expression. Preverbal experience lies beyond our field of access. We can never claim with absolute certainty that a person has actually been privileged with extraordinary experiences. Aside from the remote possibility of outright deception (usually ruled out by the context of an author's moral and religious life), we face the more serious problem that most mystical writings are not straightforwardly confessional. Christianity possesses few mystical "confessions" before the twelfth century. Those confessional writings that exist tend to translate the original experience into the universal terminology of the current religious language. How faithfully does such a universalized interpretation reflect the primary experience?

Language, especially language about the ineffable, never copies; it always creates. A perceptive reader of French mystics recently advanced the daring claim that in the modern period language has in fact become a substitute for experience.[1] Spiritual men and women, according to him, unwilling to accept the enormous spiritual loss caused by a secularized culture, attempted to compensate for it by construing a religious refuge for themselves in a highly refined and articulate mystical language. Mystical language, then, functions in a performative way, as a means for acquiring what the person lacks. Without fully ascribing to the theory, we have to admit that an already existing language has always determined the expression of the experience and, to some extent, the experience as well. Rarely appealing to the kind of "extraordinary experience" with which we identify the term "mystical," spiritual men and women try to articulate an original

1. Michel de Certeau, *La fable mystique* (Paris: Gallimard, 1982), vol. 1.

awareness of God's presence in the soul within an established linguistic frame. Avoiding any theory that tends to reduce the role of language
to a mere tool of experience, the student of mystical texts must attribute a primary significance to the words themselves. If language
mediates experience, each text possesses an intentionality of its own.
It is to this intentionality, not to inaccessibly private experience, that
we address ourselves. In doing so we fully assume that a unique
spiritual text expresses a unique manner of experiencing. But we
escape involving ourselves in insoluble problems.

Meanwhile, unavoidable questions about experience as conveyed in
the text confront us. In the first place, the basic question whether what
is described as *unio mystica* refers to an experience or, rather, to a state of
being that lies beyond consciousness altogether. Mystics suggest,
directly or indirectly, that at the peak moments of the unitive state,
consciousness itself recedes or at least comes to function in ways
incompatible with ordinary states of mind. Saint Teresa in her description of the mystical marriage mentions an ecstasy "so complete that it
seems as though the soul no longer existed."[2] Does the mystic lose
consciousness? He or she certainly appears to enter the ecstasy in full
awareness and, afterward, to remember it well enough to write clearly
about it. Hence the term "unconscious" seems inappropriate, even
though some reports refer to the unitive ecstasy as "beyond consciousness." Some commentators attempt to solve the problem by distinguishing consciousness from self-consciousness. Self-consciousness
would be temporarily lost while consciousness remains. But how could
one be at all conscious without being in some way *self*-conscious? Still,
the distinction remains useful insofar as it evokes an apparent shift of
the center of awareness from the self to a point beyond the self. A change
of this kind drastically reorients the field of consciousness. Another
solution, proposed by Joseph Maréchal in a classic essay on the psychology of ecstasy, refers to a "polarized unconsciousness," that is, a *"subcon-
sciousness* not disintegrated but gathered together and directed."[3] Yet I
wonder how such an interpretation accounts for what the sixteenth-
century Spanish mystics call an "intellectual vision," which they con-

2. Teresa of Avila, *The Interior Castle,* mansion 7, 3, trans. Allison Peers (New
York: Doubleday, 1962).
3. Joseph Maréchal, *The Psychology of the Mystics,* trans. Algar Thorold (Albany,
N.Y.: Magi Books, 1964), pp. 190, 194.

sider strictly unitive and which includes some sort of comprehensive intuition. Saint Ignatius describes such a vision in the following terms: "Without having any vision he understood — knew — many matters both spiritual and pertaining to the faith and to the realm of letters, and that with such clearness that they seemed utterly new to him. There is no possibility of setting out in detail everything he then understood. The most that he can say is that he was given so great an enlightening of mind that, if one were to put it together, all the helps he has received from God — and all the things he has learned, they would not be the equal of what he received in a single illumination."[4] Earlier, more impersonal descriptions of the unitive state display an even more clearly articulated content. Thus in the Flemish and Rhineland schools a highly complex Trinitarian theology comes to play a dominant role. Saint Teresa also reports several Trinitarian visions and so does Marie of the Incarnation.

I submit that we should distinguish the general state of union, which implies a unified vision of reality, from those ecstatic experiences that occasionally accompany it, but by no means constitute its essence. The unitive state may in fact include fewer ecstasies than the one preceding it. Saint Teresa claims that the unitive state begins with an intellectual (i.e., nonimaginary) ecstatic vision.[5] In such visions God, according to John of the Cross, touches the substance of the soul, and Teresa speaks of them as taking place "in the center of the soul." All of this suggests that the mind here enters a wholly new awareness that so much exceeds familiar forms of experiencing that the mystic is forced to turn to such odd terms as "substance," "center of the soul," "beyond consciousness."

How could the mind "experience" a reality that it declares to lie beyond the mind's measure? Consciousness here merely appears to reverberate at the impact of a reality that surpasses it. Still we would misinterpret the mystic's meaning if we considered this reality as lying "beyond" or "outside" the mind. Where knower and known are substantially united, that union no longer allows any distance for subject-object oppositions such as determine ordinary epistemic processes. The mind functions here in the different mode of being-with reality, rather than of reflecting upon it. This unique connatu-

4. Ignatius of Loyola, *Autobiography*, in *Ignatius of Loyola: The Spiritual Exercises and Selected Works*, ed. George E. Ganss, S.J. (New York: Paulist Press, 1991), p. 81.
5. Teresa of Avila, *Interior Castle*, mansion 7, 1.

rality — born of identity — between the mind and what never could be its "object" has induced the few philosophers who have given these matters serious thought to distinguish it from all other forms of human cognition. Joseph Maréchal speaks of "an intellectual intuition" — a term that his Kantian epistemology rules out for any other mode of knowing. Jacques Maritain interprets the union as the only instance of the soul directly knowing its own "substance" (within the divine substance).[6] There lies, of course, a paradox in such references to exceptional insight when we compare them to those other declarations, according to which the *unio mystica* occurs beyond consciousness. Descriptions continue to oscillate between extraordinary awareness and loss of (ordinary) consciousness.

I see no other way of reconciling those two but by assuming that the center of the mind has turned from self-consciousness to God-consciousness. The mind then becomes at once a center of presence and of absence. This interpretation appears to be confirmed by the mystic's awareness of a need to empty the self of its own content before the final state of union. Julian of Norwich writes: "No soul is at rest until it has despised as nothing [naughted] all things which are created. When it by its will has become nothing [naught] for love, to have Him who is everything, then it is able to receive spiritual rest."[7] The "naughting" of the self is the other side of unification. It obviously does not refer to a single act but to a slow and presumably painful process of self-emptying. Precisely at this point appears that "dark night" which purifies the soul, beyond its own will and ability, of attachment to itself and, by a process of "progressive unification,"[8] prepares it for a state of union. The radical reversal of attachment, the total displacement of the original center of meaning and value demanded by such a state, the mystic cannot actively achieve. His or her attachment to the self must be passively burned out, as John of the Cross expresses so powerfully in the second book of *The Dark Night of the Soul.*

Assuming, then, that the *unio mystica* consists in a state of being

6. Jacques Maritain, *Redeeming the Time,* trans. Harry L. Binsse (London: Geoffrey Bles, 1946), pp. 240-42.

7. Julian of Norwich, *Showings* (long text), vol. 5, Classics of Western Spirituality, trans. Edmund Colledge and James Walsh (New York: Paulist Press, 1978), p. 184.

8. Maréchal, *Psychology,* p. 196.

more than in a transient experience (as William James assumed in his famous four characteristics), how do we define it? In the highest "mansion," the seventh, of her *Inner Castle of the Soul,* Teresa refers to it as "an abiding place for God and a second heaven." It commences with what she calls an intellectual vision, that is, an imageless intuition during which for a brief period the mind's functions become unified while receiving a comprehensive insight into the source and coherence of all reality. Though clearly not intellectual in any discursive, rational sense, such a "vision" possesses a distinctly cognitive quality to which John of the Cross refers as a "knowledge of naked truth," that is, a "comprehending and seeing with the understanding that truths of God, whether of things that are, that have been or that will be."[9] This insight reflects a direct union with God achieved "in the substance of the soul."[10] Saint Teresa likewise refers to the union as occurring "in the deepest center of the soul, which must be where God himself dwells."[11] The final state of permanent union is characterized by an uninterrupted awareness of God's presence. That presence may not always be fully "sensed," but it remains the horizon against which all other phenomena appear. "We might compare the soul to a person who is with others in a very bright room; and then suppose that the shutters are closed so that the people are all in darkness. The light by which they can be seen has been taken away, and until it comes back, we shall be unable to see them, yet we are nonetheless aware that they are there."[12] The permanent quality of the union distinguishes this state of "spiritual marriage" from the so-called betrothal in which the feeling of presence is still punctuated by periods of absence. A divided consciousness enables the mystic to take care of ordinary duties, even to suffer and to be disturbed on one level while preserving tranquillity on another. The "center of the soul" remains untouched by what preoccupies the mind's surface. No pain or unrest enters that inner sanctuary. "A king is living in his palace: many wars are waged in his kingdom and many other distressing things happen there, but he remains where he is despite them all."[13]

9. John of the Cross, *Ascent of Mount Carmel,* trans. Allison Peers (New York: Doubleday, 1958), vol. 2, chap. 26, 2.

10. John of the Cross, *Ascent,* 2, 24, 4.

11. Teresa of Avila, *Interior Castle,* 7, 2.

12. Teresa of Avila, *Interior Castle,* 7, 2.

13. Teresa of Avila, *Interior Castle,* 7, 2.

Such highly metaphorical language evokes more questions than
it answers. Yet it is by no means arbitrary or the result of theological
indoctrination. The division between a deeper and a surface level of
the mind runs through all of Western mysticism. The great Muslim
mystic al Hallaj speaks of the transformation of the carnal *nafs* (the
animal soul) into the *rouh* (the spirit). Rabbi Eliah De Vidas distinguishes soul, spirit, and higher soul. In Christianity the distinction
between two or, more commonly, three levels of the soul appears in
several Greek Fathers, as well as in twelfth-century Cistercians and
Victorines, in thirteenth- and fourteenth-century Flemish mystics, in
sixteenth-century Spanish Carmelites, in seventeenth-century French
masters, and in eighteenth-century Quietists. Richard of St. Victor
has expressed it with surpassing precision: "We must not understand
a twofold substance by these two words [soul and spirit], but when
we distinguish between the twin powers of the same essence, the
higher is called spirit, the lower soul. In this distinction the soul and
that which is animal remains below, but the spirit and that which is
spiritual flies upward. That which is of the body and subject to cor-
ruption perishes and as a dead body falls back into itself and below
its nature. That which is subtle and purified ascends upward."[14] Precisely the division of the mind here postulated enables the mystic to
combine a contemplative life with one of active service. Yet in describing the two attitudes as being juxtaposed one risks missing the
real nature of the case. For one is not superimposed to the other: the
two intimately collaborate and reinforce each other.

Among the outstanding qualities of the religious attitude we must
certainly count its remarkable ability to integrate life, to achieve unity
within the divergent complexity of opposite tendencies. The mystical
state, far from diminishing this synthetic capacity, enhances the psy-
chic powers of concentration. Precisely in this respect a mysticizing
philosophy differs from a genuine personal or communal mystical
inspiration. Evelyn Underhill clearly perceived how much the mystical union strengthens a person's capacity to fulfill his or her given
or assumed task. She wrote: "It is the peculiarity of the unitive life
that it is often lived, in its highest and most perfect form, in the world;

14. Richard of St. Victor, *De exterminatione mali*, pt. 3, chap. 18, p. 267, trans. in
Elmer O'Brien, *The Varieties of Mystical Experience* (New York: Holt, Rinehart, Winston, 1964), p. 133.

and exhibits its works before the eyes of men. . . . The spirit of man having at last come to full consciousness of reality, completes the circle of Being; and returns to fertilize those levels of existence from which it sprang. Hence the enemies of mysticism . . . are here confronted very often by the disagreeable spectacle of the mystic as a pioneer of humanity, a sharply intuitive and painfully practical person: an artist, a discoverer, a religious or social reformer, a national hero, a 'great active' among the saints."[15]

Even a work as unworldly as *The Cloud of Unknowing* emphatically stresses the spiritual fecundity of the contemplative life. Having come to participate in God's life, the contemplative also comes to share God's life-giving love.[16] Mystical marriage invariably leads to spiritual parenthood. Mystics have never shied away from the paradox that the "highest" results in "the humblest." While the third degree of love according to Richard of St. Victor glorifies the soul in the likeness of God, in the fourth, supreme degree, she descends from the lonely peaks of contemplation to practice charity in the lowly world of men. "He who ascends to this degree of charity is truly in the state of love that can say: 'I am made all things to all men that I might save all.'"[17] We know the wonders this conversion to "the humblest" achieved in such mystics as Francis of Assisi, Catherine of Siena, or Ignatius of Loyola. The seventeenth-century French Ursuline nun, Marie of the Incarnation, who spent the latter part of her life in Quebec, has left a unique witness of this need to transform contemplation into chari-table action. In the 1654 *Relation* of her spiritual journey she distin-guishes thirteen stages of prayer of which the spiritual marriage is only the seventh — a surprising position to take for one who had been trained in the spiritual classics. In traditional theory the mystical ascent culminates in the spiritual marriage. Apparently Marie felt that "the state" of union which she herself declares to be permanent remains incomplete until it has fully incorporated the various active modes in which it finds its expression: only through them does the state of union become complete.

15. Evelyn Underhill, *Mysticism* (New York: Dutton, 1961), p. 414.

16. Harvey D. Egan, S.J., *Christian Mysticism: The Future of a Tradition* (New York: Pueblo, 1984), p. 96.

17. Richard of St. Victor, *The Four Degrees of Passionate Love,* in *Richard of St. Victor: Select Writings on Contemplation,* ed. and trans. Clare Kirchberger (London: Faber & Faber, 1957).

A purely negative theology, of course, would never result in such a commitment to the finite. Yet in Christianity all unitive mysticism moves beyond a mere denial of the finite. To be sure, the mystic upon entering that union finds the finite incommensurate to God's Being. But as he or she is admitted to participate in that Being the mystic ceases to compare the finite with the infinite. Instead, she or he takes the finite on its own terms and asserts the divine meaning of the finite as it remains within God's own Being. Thus the divine manifestation once allowed to shine in its own light illuminates the real in its entirety. The inherence of the finite within God's own creative act led Ignatius of Loyola to conclude his *Spiritual Exercises* with an exhortation to consider "how God dwells in all creatures," that is, how the finite exists within the infinite. The *unio mystica* restores a divine meaning to the finite that was absent in the early stage of spiritual ascent and that negative theology permanently ignores. The *unio mystica* overcomes the separation between God and the creature. God is not opposed to anything, since he integrates all things in his divine Being. For the mystic, transcendence ceases to consist in a negation of the finite. Instead, God appears as the ultimate dimension of the finite, the inaccessible within the accessible.

Though the state of union always implies some reintegration of the created world with God, few have consistently attempted to justify the return to the finite through a participation in God's own inner life. One who did so in a most powerful theological synthesis was Ruusbroec. For him the relations among the "Persons" of the Trinity form the basis of the mystic's view of the finite within the infinite. When God unites himself "without means" to the soul, he surpasses all intermediacy of created grace and virtue. In that encounter the soul loses itself in "a state of darkness in which all contemplatives blissfully lose their way and are never again able to find themselves in a creaturely way."[18] Yet in this blissful union the soul comes to share the dynamics of God's inner life, a life not only of rest and darkness, but also of creative activity and light. The contemplative admitted to this union is granted to follow the outflowing movement of the Godhead. He participates in the eternal Word as it proceeds from the divine silence, containing all creation within itself. Union with God, then,

---

18. John Ruusbroec, *The Spiritual Espousals,* trans. James Wiseman, Classics of Western Spirituality (New York: Paulist Press, 1985), p. 147.

for Ruusbroec, means union with God's self-expression — the internal one of the Word as well as the external one of creation. Partaking in the divine rhythm of contraction and expansion (expressed in the doctrine of the Trinity), the state of union alternates active charity with contemplative solitude. Sharing what Ruusbroec calls the "life-giving fruitfulness of the divine nature," the contemplative accompanies God's own move from hiddenness to manifestation, within the identity of God's own life.[19]

Mystical theology has traditionally distinguished the interpersonal unity of mind *(unitas spiritus)* from the ontological or substantial unity *(unitas indistinctionis).* Yet mystics tend to use interpersonal language for expressing the state of union, while some of the most articulate exponents of love mysticism (Hadewych, John of the Cross, Teresa of Avila) do not hesitate to use the terminology of substantial union. Evelyn Underhill distinguishes spiritual marriage from that state of deification whereby the self becomes absorbed by the Absolute. Yet immediately she qualifies her description of the latter by adding: "The personal and emotional aspect of man's relation with his Source is also needed if that which he means by 'union with God' is to be even partially expressed. Hence, even the most 'transcendental' mystic is constantly compelled to fall back on the language of love in the endeavor to express the content of the metaphysical raptures: and forced in the end to acknowledge that the perfect union of Lover and Beloved cannot be suggested in the precise and arid terms of religious philosophy."[20]

Ruusbroec's most significant contribution to this dialectic of union and communion consists in having shown how the mystical life develops within the initially given, ontological unity of the soul with God. Rather than reflecting what the soul is from the start, the mystical ascent surpasses the mere awareness of an already present, ontological union. Contemplative love transforms the soul's virtual inexistence in the divine Logos into a living reality. For Ruusbroec, the unified mind, beyond being a state of consciousness, functions as an active lever of being.

The mystic, then, emerges as the *homo religiosus* par excellence, the

19. The reader interested in this rhythm may be referred to Louis Dupré, *The Common Life* (New York: Crossroads, 1984).

20. Underhill, *Mysticism,* p. 425.

one who recognizes that reality remains incomplete until it becomes reunited with its source. All monotheist religion aims at some union with God. But while to the ordinary believer this union remains mostly a spiritual or a moral ideal that has no impact upon the structure of the real, for the mystic it brings reality itself to completion and, as such, becomes the intrinsic telos of all being. To the question — What is the specific being of mind? — the mystic answers, "That dynamic power without which being cannot fully be." All mystics, explicitly or implicitly, have held some variation of Rabbi Nahman's amazing assertion that God has created the world in order to enable Israel to return to its source: without that return the world itself would be left in a diminished state of being. To the mystic, the cosmic structure appears forever waiting for a completion which only the God-loving mind can convey. At the opposite end of the static metaphysics, according to which being is and becoming is not, the mystical mind views itself as driven by a higher power that destines it to be the unifying link between what is only in part and what is wholly and unqualifiedly real. In the process of fulfilling this function the mind moves from a lower or more superficial level of consciousness to a "higher" or "deeper" level in which mind turns into being. Though aiming at supreme rest above commotion, the mystic is occupied in conveying definitive meaning and value to a restless world.

Viewed in this light the question that provoked much discussion among theologians from the twelfth to the fourteenth century — whether the final state of the contemplative process, the *unio mystica,* is cognitive or affective in nature — loses much of its meaning. To call it cognitive or affective is to treat an essentially unified and unifying consciousness as a divided, oppositional one. Unless consciousness be both cognitive and affective, it misses the very wholeness characteristic of the final union. The mystic understands the real as a totality of which the mind constitutes an integral, dynamic part. Of course, distinctions and emphases remain, even in the *unio mystica.* Differences between one mystic and another, between one school and another, even within the same religious tradition, continue to influence the very nature of the union. Nevertheless mystics constantly break through existing theological divisions, in order to stress the unity of love and cognition. Gregory the Great's formula *amor ipse notitia* ("love itself is knowledge") provided Western contemplatives with a basis for affirming, again and again, that the highest love includes the supreme knowledge.

Since all love implies duality, it is significant that even mystics who advocate a substantial union often resort to the language of love. Should we not hold the dynamic quality, so essential to the mystical process, responsible for this persistence of an erotic terminology? While knowledge essentially consists in an awareness of what is, love must attain its goal slowly and often painfully. Hence all mystics, including those who presuppose the ontological presence of the soul in God, regard the mystical union as completing a dynamic process for which the initial presence merely establishes the necessary condition. In choosing the language of love in spite of its inherent inadequacy, mystics translate into theory an experience that, for most of them, consists in a process.

Yet a second factor appears to have influenced the priority of love. Many have assumed it, though few have dared to express it. It is the idea that love changes God himself. The Flemish mystic Richard of St. Victor, one of the first in the Christian tradition to mention it, boldly asserts that love "wounds" God.[21] Once we have become alerted to the idea we find it implied in the writings of many mystics. Teresa of Avila becomes unintelligible unless we assume that her divine Lover responds in accordance with the way her words affect him. The same holds true for Thérèse of Lisieux and Marie of the Incarnation. Angelus Silesius succinctly expressed this mutual relationship:

There are but you and I, and when we two are not
The heavens will collapse, God will no more be God.

God shelters me as much as I do shelter Him,
His Being I sustain, sustained I am therein.[22]

Among love mystics only the Quietists (Molinos, Guyon, Fénelon) form a possible exception to this rule. For them the highest love consists in acquiring an attitude of total acceptance of God's immutability. Precisely this position, however, caused the movement no end of troubles with authorities suspicious of an ideal so contrary to human inclination. We may conclude, I believe, that the language of

21. Richard of St. Victor, *De gradibus caritatis*, P.L. 196, 1023b.
22. Angelus Silesius, *The Cherubinic Wanderer*, trans. Maria Shrady, Classics of Western Spirituality (New York: Paulist Press, 1986), pp. 65, 43.

love and devotion, despite its inherent dualism, has provided Christians with a much-needed discourse for expressing the dynamic quality so essential to the mystical process. Many mystics have articulated the goal and final stages of a loving communion with God in terms of substantial union, which are hardly compatible with the duality of love. Likewise, mystics who assume the idea of a substantial union see themselves forced to have recourse to a language of love in order to express the growing nature of that union. The language of love among humans is the most obvious, for Christians perhaps the only, available for that purpose.

Spiritual Life in a Secular Age

In the eighteenth century, the idea of God ceased to be a vital concern for our intellectual culture. Almost without transition, deism had merged into a practical atheism. In the nineteenth century, the secularized consciousness, no longer satisfied with a *de facto* absence of any meaningful transcendence, attempted to convert its attitude into a *de jure,* justified one. Thus originated the virulent antitheisms of scientific positivism, sociological structuralism, and axiological humanism. These antitheist trends have survived into our own day, yet they no longer dominate the religious situation of the present. Today's atheism by and large considers its position sufficiently secure to feel no need for defining itself through a negative relation to faith, nor does it exclude the range of religious experience. Indeed, it has extended its territory to include the significant, yet previously neglected, area of spiritual phenomena. It certainly has abandoned the nineteenth-century dream of a purely scientific humanism. As a rule, it no longer expects an integral worldview from science, and it is even beginning to abandon the previous identification of science with human progress. In short, contemporary humanism is less polemical, more comprehensive, but also more thoroughly immanent than that of the recent past.

Strangely enough, this humanism beyond atheism was prepared by the three men we most commonly associate with modern atheism, Freud, Marx, and Nietzsche. These "prophets of suspicion," though leaving no doubt about their personal atheism, nevertheless felt that the future was moving beyond this polemical attitude. Freud conceded that the neurotic character of faith, which he was satisfied to have scientifically established, did not per se preclude the possibility of an

131

objective truth; but to search the foundations of such a negative possibility, after an exhaustive positive interpretation had already been given of all religion's features, did not appear to him to be a very useful enterprise. As he tolerantly informed his readers: "Just as no one can be forced to believe, so no one can be forced to disbelieve. But do not let us be satisfied with deceiving ourselves that arguments like these take us along the road of correct thinking. If ever there was a case of a lame excuse we have it here. Ignorance is ignorance; no right to believe anything can be derived from it."[1]

What appears more polemically atheistic than Marxism, both in its actual policies and in the very words of Marx upon which these policies are founded? Yet even a superficial acquaintance with Marx's mature theory suffices to convince one of the humanist trend of his thought. To be sure, Marx set out as a belligerent antitheist. With Feuerbach, he saw religion as a person's projection of his or her own nature into an ideal sphere that alienated the believer from his/her human attributes. But Marx, detecting in this projection a more fundamental estrangement between the individual and society, felt less and less induced to fight the enchanting shadow image instead of the harsh reality that caused it. "Atheism as a denial of this unreality [of God] is no longer meaningful, for atheism is a *negation of God* and seeks to assert by this negation the *existence of man.* Socialism no longer requires such a roundabout method; it begins from the theoretical and practical sense perception of man and nature as essential beings. It is positive human self-consciousness; no longer a self-consciousness attained through the negation of religion."[2] Atheism is itself no more than an ideology, an idle and ill-directed theoretical attitude that only drains much-needed energy away from the battle for a true humanization. The communist position rejects both theism and atheism. "Communism begins where atheism begins, but atheism is at the outset still far from being *communism;* indeed it is still for the most part an abstraction. The philanthropy of atheism is at first only a philosophical

---

1. Sigmund Freud, *The Future of an Illusion,* vol. 21 in the *Complete Psychological Works,* trans. under the direction of James Strachey (London: Hogarth Press, 1961), p. 32.

2. Karl Marx, *Economic and Philosophic Manuscripts of 1888,* in Marx-Engels *Collected Works* (New York: International Publishers, 1975), 3:306 (slightly changed).

philanthropy, whereas that of communism is at once real and oriented action."[3]

Axiological humanism has basically followed the same evolutionary path since Nietzsche so boldly declared genuine freedom to be incompatible with the idea of a value-creating God. I know that Nietzsche and most of his followers as late as Sartre formulated this thesis in antitheistic polemical phrases. But they advocated something different and far more radical: a totally self-sufficient humanism, which goes well beyond these polemics. Maurice Merleau-Ponty articulated the new attitude when he refused to be called an atheist, because atheism is still "an inverted act of faith."[4] The humanist must start not with the denial of God, but with the affirmation of the human, the sole source of meaning.

Despite the phraseology, scientific, Marxist, and axiological humanisms have mostly abandoned their antireligious stand for an attitude of all-comprehensive openness that, instead of fighting the values traditionally represented by religion, attempts to incorporate them into more accommodating syntheses. To the extent that these attempts have succeeded, they have changed the perspective of our culture and have replaced religion in what used to be its unique function of integrating all of life. For many of our contemporaries, religion has been reduced to an experience, one among others, occasionally powerful, but not sufficiently so to draw the rest of their existence into its orbit.

Of course, the distinction between the sacred areas of existence and the more profane ones occurred very early in our culture. I do not doubt that the increasing complexity of our lives made such a distinction indispensable. Yet nowhere before have profane matters become secular — that is, entirely independent of what once was their transcendent life source. In our own age, science, social structures, and morality, having developed into full, albeit purely immanent, forms of humanism, have lost virtually all need for the public support of religion. Our contemporaries, particularly the young and the educated, the ones most susceptible to cultural change, have to a large extent resigned themselves to a fragmented worldview. The old battles between science and faith marked the final attempts to find a unified

---

3. Marx-Engels, *Collected Works,* 3:297.
4. Maurice Merleau-Ponty, *Eloge de la philosophie* (Paris, 1953), p. 59.

vision in which either the religious or the secular had to prevail. Most of us now regard those controversies as dated; believers, as well as unbelievers, have moderated their claims. Far from "explaining" everything, believers now admit, faith may not even be able to reconcile all of its claims with other, partial "world" views by which they live. Today the famed earthquake of Lisbon that so shocked Voltaire would cause hardly a ripple among the faithful — not because it creates no problems, but because they have given up looking for theological solutions in all domains of life.

Highly visible and audible fundamentalist movements are attempting to turn this tide of secularization. Deliberately closing themselves to the beliefs and values of their age, their followers hope to reestablish the lost objective certainty by simply denying cultural changes any religious significance. Their presence is felt in the violently antimodernist revolutions that shake the world of Islam and in the aggressive regressiveness of fundamentalist power lobbies. But some of this separatism also inspires groups and individuals who appear perfectly attuned to the rhythms of modern life and feel no desire of turning the clock back. By leading lives of "hidden interiority," they manage to disconnect spiritual life from the onslaught of the prevailing culture. Yet their schizoid attitude is bound to become untenable before long. This desperate attempt to isolate the secular reveals an inability to incorporate it in some manner into the relation to the transcendent. Such inability is itself an entirely new phenomenon. The premodern opposition between the sacred and the profane did not obstruct the ability to relate *all* facets of human existence to a transcendent ultimacy. In our present culture "the sacred," wherever it is still experienced, has lost the power directly to integrate the rest of life. We are now witnessing the unprecedented phenomenon of a religion that is rapidly becoming desacralized. The "experience of the sacred," with which phenomenologists since Rudolph Otto have readily identified religion, can no longer be considered normative of the religion of our time. Few of our contemporaries connect their faith with the kind of private or communal sacred experiences described by Otto, Van der Leeuw, or Eliade. To be sure, intensive religious experiences continue to exist, but they have become the exception rather than the rule, and happen mostly to those who have already, and in different ways, actively committed themselves to transcendent reality. Generally speaking, their attitude owes more to personal reflection and deliberate choice than to direct experience.

Of course, everyone who decides to live religiously does so on the basis of *some* experience. Faith — as we understand that word (an understanding that, I suspect, is strongly colored by a Christian outlook) — has at all times consisted of both experience *and* decision. What uniquely distinguishes our present situation is the nature of the experience. Direct and self-interpretative in the past, it is now ambiguous and open to a multiplicity of interpretations. In our time, the religious interpretation comes as a result of further reflection, and only rarely with the experience itself. Since the interpretation remains separate from the experience, the doubt about its correctness can be resolved only by a subsequent, full commitment to it. Hence, the experience receives its definitive meaning only in this final, voluntary act of assent. Newman detached the assent of faith from its inconclusive premises. The current cultural condition has extended the gap well beyond the logical level. There has, of course, always been a void between an immanent awareness and the affirmation of a transcendent reality. But past experience was sufficiently supported by the surrounding culture to carry the believer across the void by his or her participation in an objective communion of faith. Experience, interpretation, and decision occurred in one continuous act. That connection today is broken. An ambiguous experience justifies the believer's faith as well as the unbeliever's unbelief.

Let me illustrate this by a typical example, the awareness of radical contingency. This awareness, almost universal in a world whose awesome complexity and unimaginable vastness modern science has revealed, discourages many from probing beyond the mystery that science itself discloses. To them, the unpromising quest for *ultimate* intelligibility merely detracts from the urgent and immediate task of exercising rational control over their world. For others, the mystery of inexplicable gratuitousness points to a transcendent horizon. Clearly, the interpretation here colors the experience. What makes some people favor one interpretation and others the opposite? Social tradition? But this is precisely the factor that has lost much of its original impact in a society that is itself pluralistic and where even the ties with the immediate family have ceased to function as ideological bonds. The orthodox are right in referring to "grace," a choice for which no clear logical, social, or psychological reasons are available.

But, of course, the student of religion is not allowed to invoke one unknown factor in order to explain all others.

Religious men and women will continue to attribute a "sacred" quality to persons, objects, and events closely connected with their relation to the transcendent. But they will do so because they *hold* them sacred, not because they *perceive* them as sacred. In the end it is their decision and/or grace, more than any direct experience, that determines what they will *hold* sacred. "The religious person embraces only those doctrines which cast light upon his inner awareness, joins only those groups to which he or she feels moved from within, and performs only those acts which express his self-transcendence."[5] The external and institutional elements of religion seem to have been reduced to an instrumental role. I do not mean to predict that religion will ever be without communally established symbols, but rather that those who maintain a religious attitude tend to use institutions and interpret traditional symbols on the basis of their *personal* needs and preferences. This undoubtedly gives religion a somewhat eclectic and — for those who judge it by past objective standards — arbitrary appearance. In an unexpected way, the religious impulse has now started to incorporate the religious pluralism that, to a considerable degree, triggered the secularist crisis of the modern age. The existence of such phenomena as Christian Zen, Jews for Jesus, and Calvinist monasteries signals a wholly new way of coming to grips with transcendence in which the center of gravity has shifted from the objective institution to the subjective decision.

In the modern world, religion no longer exercises its integrating function — so essential to its survival — primarily by means of ecclesial power or discipline, or even by means of doctrinal authority. Increasingly the basis of authority has come to lie in the personal decision to *adopt* a traditional doctrine and to *use* it for guidance and integration of the various aspects of social and private conduct. It is not that believers have replaced doctrine by an eclectic *choice* of symbols. An arbitrary choice of signs of ultimate meaning is indicative of an advanced secularism, not of a serious religious attitude. Yet even genuine religion today differs from the past in that it integrates from

---

5. Louis Dupré, *Transcendent Selfhood* (New York: Seabury Press, 1976), pp. 29-30. See also Peter Berger, *The Heretical Imperative* (New York: Doubleday, 1979), pp. 32ff.

within rather than from without, even when it continues to uphold the commitment to a particular doctrine and cult. Their authority, however, becomes operative only after and to the extent that they have been personally accepted and interiorized. Spiritual men and women of the modern age are, and will be in the foreseeable future, recognizable as Christians, Jews, or Muslims, yet the increasing emphasis on the personal decision is likely to make them less exclusive in their doctrinal allegiances.

Nor does the shift toward a personal decision transform religion into a purely individualist affair. To be sure, today's believers must first decide which, if any, faith they accept, and to what degree they are able to embrace its principles and norms. But having once opted for a particular faith (most likely a variety of the one in which they were raised), they readily join their efforts with those of fellow believers in implementing its religious ideals. How broadly or narrowly they interpret that faith may not affect their common effort and worship in the future any more than at present.

It is precisely the private and reflective nature of religion in a secularized culture that explains its inward trend, as well as the present interest in mystical literature. The latter may appear especially paradoxical at a time when direct religious experience is perhaps less prevalent than ever before. But what attracts the modern believer to the masters of spiritual life is, I think, less affinity of disposition than the fact that in an atheist culture there is nowhere to turn *but* inwardly. The mystics start their spiritual journey from within, and that is the only place where the believer *must* begin, whether he wants to or not. But a major obstacle arises at once, for what the believer encounters in himself is the same absence that surrounds him. His own heart remains as silent as the world in which the creatures have ceased to speak in sacred tongues. Yet it is precisely in the deliberate confrontation with this inner silence that I detect the true significance of the believer's current urge toward a spiritual life. For only after having confronted his own atheism can the believer hope to restore the vitality of his religion. The masters of spiritual life — and they alone — have been able to convey a positive meaning to what Simone Weil so aptly called that sacred "sense of absence." If fully lived through, the emptiness of one's own heart may turn into a powerful cry for the One who is not there. It is the contradiction of a simultaneous presence and absence. "I am quite sure that there is a God, in the sense that I am quite sure my love is not illusory. I am quite sure that there is not a God, in the sense that I am quite sure nothing real can be anything like what I am able to conceive when I pronounce this word." Here, the very godlessness of the world is invested with religious meaning, and a transcendent dimension opens up in this encounter with a world that has lost its divine presence. Thus the believer learns that God is entirely beyond his reach, that God is not an object but an absolute demand, that to accept God is not to accept a "giver," but a Giving. As in the night of St. John of the Cross, the night of absence, intensely experienced and accepted, becomes the meeting place between the soul and divine transcendence, a transcendence not perceived as a remote first cause, but as the transcendence of a God who has "emptied himself into the world, transformed his substance in the blind mechanism of the world, a God who dies in the inconsolable pits of human affliction."[6]

The religious consciousness of absence has its roots in earlier spiritual traditions. The intensive encounter with God has always summoned humans to take leave of the familiar words and concepts and to venture out into a desert of unlimited and unexplored horizons. The oldest and purest Buddhist doctrine proposed no other ideal than the attainment of total emptiness. Of "God" there is no question; emptiness itself becomes the space of transcendence. The monk must remain silent, yet silently he thanks the nameless source. Nor does the Samkhya Hindu feel the need for an idea of God to carry his awareness of what can have no name. Christianity, the religion of the Word, of God as manifest, has no room for an a-theist piety as such. (The atheism of some recent theologians is intrinsically bound to remain a heterodox, marginal phenomenon.) But even in the religion of manifestation, those who engage upon a serious spiritual journey invariably begin their pilgrimage by leaving the familiar names behind.

Since the third century, the mystical tradition of Christianity has recognized a theology in which all language is reduced to silence. In his *Mystical Theology*, Pseudo-Dionysius, the sixth-century Syrian monk, teaches that the state of spiritual perfection consists in being united with what lies beyond all cognition. "Into this Dark beyond all light, we pray to come and, unseeing and unknowing to see and

---

6. Susan A. Taubes, "The Absent God," in *Toward a New Christianity*, ed. Thomas J. .J. Altizer (New York: Harcourt, Brace and World, 1967), p. 116.

to know Him that is beyond seeing and beyond knowing precisely by not seeing, by not knowing."[7] This mysticism of negation culminated in fourteenth-century Rhineland. Thus Eckhart writes about the place where the soul meets with God: "When I existed in the core, the soil, the river, the source of the Godhead, no one asked me where I was going or what I was doing. There was no one there to ask me, but the moment I emerged, the world of creatures began to shout: 'God.' . . . Thus creatures speak of god — but why do they not mention the Godhead? Because there is only unity in the Godhead and there is nothing to talk about."[8]

Clearly, a negation such as Eckhart's or that of the *Cloud of Unknowing* did not emerge from a weakened religious consciousness. Quite the opposite, it emerged from a more intensive awareness of a transcendent presence — precisely what is missing in our contemporaries. Yet my point is not to compare two entirely different mentalities. Rather, it is to show that if the believer, who shares in fact, if not in principle, the practical atheism of his entire culture, is left no choice but to vitalize this negative experience and to confront his feeling of God's absence, he may find himself on the very road walked by spiritual pilgrims in more propitious times. What was once the arduous route traveled only by a religious elite is now, in many instances, the only one still open to us. To be sure, not all believers of our age are spiritual men or women, nor need they be, but to those who *are,* religion will continue to be an integrating power of life. The desert of modern atheism provides the only space in which most of them are forced to encounter the transcendent. It is a desert that in prayerful attention may be converted into the solitude of contemplation — a solitude that Thomas Merton wrote of as not something outside us, not an absence of people or of sound, but an abyss opening up in the center of the soul, an abyss created by a hunger and thirst and sorrow and poverty and desire.[9] Our age has created an emptiness that for the serious God-seeker attains a religious significance. The mysticism of negation provides us with an

7. P. G. Migne, 3:1925; in *Varieties of Mystical Experience,* trans. Elmer O'Brien (New York: Holt, Rinehart, Winston, 1964), p. 83.

8. Johannes Eckhart, "Nolite Timere," in *Meister Eckhart: A Modern Translation,* trans. Raymond B. Blakney (New York: Harper and Brothers, 1957), p. 225.

9. Thomas Merton, *Seeds of Contemplation* (New York: Dell, 1958), pp. 51-52.

ideal model. The affirmation of God is rarely still the center of our search for transcendence.

Yet, unless the modern believer in some manner overcomes the pure negation, he or she has not fully surpassed the secular atheism of the age. Even a religion of silence, such as Buddhism, moves beyond absence, however strongly it may refuse to name the transcendent. Nirvana is a purely negative concept only to the outsider. To those who live it, it is, in the words of one monk, "unspeakable bliss." Much less can traditions that so strongly emphasize the intrinsic value of the finite, as do Christianity and Judaism, tolerate their spiritual theology to remain purely negative. Christian mystics have commonly admitted some kind of theological negation, but somehow, they have all succeeded in moving beyond it. The dialectic seems to have developed somewhat in the following way. The same religious dynamism that drove them to become detached from the finite as being incommensurate with the infinite, next compelled them to abandon their own, still finite negation, which separated the creature from God, and to adopt a divine prespective in which the finite and infinite remain united in God. In this perspective, transcendence, rather than constituting the opposition between finite and infinite, reveals the divine essence of the finite and, with it, the emanational nature of God's Being. Thus, the final word about God is not "otherness," but "identity." God is the ultimate dimension of the real. So Ignatius of Loyola, at the end of his *Spiritual Exercises,* invites the exercitant who has previously renounced the creaturely world to consider now "how God dwells in all creatures." Similarly, John of the Cross, after having first denied any proportion between God and the creatures, reasserts their unity. Even Eckhart's negation of an analogy between God and the creatures results in a new analogy, based not on similarity, but on partial identity.

At present we are merely considering how this complex movement of reaffirmation can still be achieved in an age that has lost the very idea of God. Clearly, for that purpose to succeed, it does not suffice to embrace the finite as if it were infinite. Abolishing the distinction between one and the other can merely result in an aesthetic pantheism incompatible with the transcendence so essential to all genuine religion. What actually happens appears to be this: the spiritual person comes to view the world in a different perspective. Underneath ordinary reality he or she recognizes another dimension. At the very core of each creature, the contemplative finds an otherness that com-

pels him or her to allow it to be itself and to abstain from the conquering, objectifying attitude that we commonly adopt. This does not
reveal a new idea of God; rather, it allows reality to reveal itself. But
that requires a decisive break with the prevailing approach to the
creaturely reality, which stands mostly under the sign of power and
which lies at the root of our present loss of transcendence. A genuine
recognition of transcendence requires more than a decision. It presupposes a fundamental attitude toward reality. Once it disintegrates,
it cannot be replaced by a readily available equivalent, as we do when
replacing an inadequate concept by a more adequate one. It has to be
rebuilt from the bottom up. The first task here is not one of creating
a more viable system (if that were sufficient, theology would have
solved our problems long ago), but of a different outlook on the real.
It is hard to describe what does not (yet) exist. But I can think of no
better characterization than the one implied in the Latin term *pietas,*
an obedient attention to possible messages, or the one Simone Weil
has appropriately defined as waiting in expectation. We must first
remove the principal obstacle to the perception of the transcendent
dimension of the real. We must not expect to come up with a new
name for the emerging transcendent, but only to acquire a new perceptiveness for detecting it. We can hardly hope to move beyond
negative theology as long as no specifically religious realm of experience, as the "sacred" was in the past, exists for us. The worldliness of
contemporary experience tends to erase the traditional distinction
between the sacred and the profane.

But if the distinction largely vanishes, does not traditional religion
likewise disappear? What happens to the "positive" elements of faith, to
revelation, sacraments, church? In advocating a new attitude, are we, in
fact, not proposing a new religion? Is any room left for those specific
elements that make a particular faith Christian or Jewish? Or must we
admit that these declining faiths are in fact doomed to total extinction,
even among spiritual men and women? Does the inevitably "worldly"
character of spiritual life in this age leave us no alternative but some
nondenominational religion of reason? I think not: the fundamental
models of traditional religion remain available and mysteriously continue
to appeal to our secular contemporaries. One might object that, to accept
them, one must already be a "believer," and how can anyone be a
religious believer without a preliminary commitment to a distinctly
perceived, transcendent reality? The answer is that the modern believer

must first *discover* the model of his or her belief to be existentially meaningful before being able to accept it as transcendent. It has become nearly impossible to establish the divine authority of revelation before the potential believer admits the significance of the message, for that authority itself is most under question. The existential significance must at least in some measure be established before dogmatic concepts become acceptable. I am not claiming, as Christian apologists in the nineteenth century occasionally did, that Christ's significance *proved* his divinity, and hence legitimated the entire Christian faith. Apart from its obvious logical flaw, that argument begs the most crucial issue in the modern problematic — whether the idea of transcendence itself is meaningful. Faith will, more than ever, remain what it always was: a leap beyond experience. But, contrary to what fideists often claim, that leap was never blind. It always led from partial insight to total acceptance. The same structure is maintained today when the "believer," dissatisfied with the shallowness of a closed, secular world, abandons the conquering, grasping attitude for a more receptive one.

Nor would it be correct to assume that the community loses its role in the highly personal religion of the present, for as soon as the believer adopts a model, such as Christ is for Christians, he or she joins a community of like-minded individuals which, in some way, renders this ideal model a *present* reality. By providing the believer with sacraments, Scriptures, and a whole system of representations, the religious community enables the individual to integrate his or her private spiritual life within a living communion.

Is all of this more than a theological adjustment to different circumstances, of which there have been so many in the course of history? I think it is! Theology articulates a particular vision of the transcendent. The articulation is occasionally challenged, but the vision seldom changes. In the present situation, the very reality of the transcendent is at stake, more than its specific conceptualization. The very possibility of a relation to the transcendent in the modern world has come under fire. Theology in the past could count on some *direct* experience of the sacred. Such an experience can no longer be taken for granted. The religious attitude of Western men and women has largely become what it never was before, a matter of existential choice. If they *believe,* they do so not because of an inherited tradition and seldom because of a direct religious experience, but rather because of an accumulation of experiences confronting them with various

choices, one of which they must make their own by a personal decision. Thence the joining of a religious community, the reception of
sacraments, even the acceptance of the doctrine established in that
community, have come to depend on deliberate decision. They will
soon turn into empty shells unless they are constantly replenished by
a rather intensive and deliberate spiritual awareness. The search for a
deeper spiritual life, then, means more than a passing phenomenon
on today's religious scene; it is a movement for religious survival. For
without the support of a spiritually sustained personal decision, a faith
opposed by the surrounding culture and constantly under attack in
the believer's own heart is doomed to die.

Instead of the traditional distinction between sacred objects, persons, and events, and profane ones, spiritual men and women in the
future will regard existence increasingly as an indivisible unity,
wholly worldly and self-sufficient, yet at the same time they will be
aware of a mysterious depth dimension that demands attention and
that they allow to direct their basic attitude to their life. They may
start from the negative experience of life lived in a secular environment, deprived of a transcendent meaning. Yet less than ever, I
suspect, will they remain satisfied with a negative attitude toward
their worldly and social environment. Theirs will rather be a spirituality of world-affirmation, a mystique of creation that discovers a
transcendent dimension in a fundamental engagement to a world
and a human community perceived as totally autonomous and totally
dependent.

Index of Authors